FEEDING THE FIRE

FEEDING THE FIRE

RECIPES & STRATEGIES FOR BETTER BARBECUE & GRILLING

JOE CARROLL & NICK FAUCHALD

Photographs by William Hereford

ARTISAN

NEW YORK

Library of Congress Cataloging-in-Publication Data

Carroll, Joe (Restaurateur)
    Feeding the fire / Joe Carroll and Nick Fauchald.
        pages cm
    Includes index.
    ISBN 978-1-57965-557-0
1. Barbecuing. I. Fauchald, Nick. II. Title.
TX840.B3C337 2015
641.7'6—dc23   2014035876

Design by Toni Tajima
Food styling by Rebekah Peppler

Artisan books are available at special discounts when purchased in bulk for premiums and sales promotions as well as for fund-raising or educational use. Special editions or book excerpts also can be created to specification. For details, contact the Special Sales Director at the address below, or send an e-mail to specialmarkets@workman.com.

Published by Artisan
A division of Workman Publishing Company, Inc.
225 Varick Street
New York, NY 10014-4381
artisanbooks.com

Published simultaneously in Canada by Thomas Allen & Son, Limited

Printed in China

First printing, May 2015

10 9 8 7 6 5 4 3 2 1

TO CORA AND DANTE

CONTENTS

FOREWORD

BY STEPHEN STARR

IT'S NO STRETCH to say that Joe Carroll is a rare breed among restaurateurs. I'd go so far as to say that he's actually a rare breed among people.

In both of my lives—that is, my old life in the music business and my current life in the restaurant world—I have very rarely come across a successful person whose vision and inspiration come entirely from within. Joe is one of those guys. He's the type who doesn't study trends, but instead sees promise in ideas that nobody else has ever considered; the type who sits down and writes a hit song without ever having listened to anyone else's music. It's an enviable gift. (And believe me, some twenty years and forty restaurants into my career, I do envy it.)

Joe is my partner in Philadelphia's Fette Sau, the barbecue restaurant he dreamed up and first opened in Brooklyn to great acclaim. The praise for the food and the character of the restaurant is justly earned, though I think what people really respond to at Fette Sau is more than just great barbecue and savvy art direction. I'd say it's the same thing that I responded to when I first met Joe in 2012, and that's his innate ability to grow one small, well-defined idea into something with outsize impact. His restaurants have been more than a breath of fresh air in the Brooklyn and Philadelphia food worlds; they have been game-changers on a national level.

Beyond the great idea, past the initial flash of brilliance, what we see with Joe is an almost anthropological commitment to the culture of the food, an exhaustive understanding of the details that make a restaurant come together. (How else to explain how a kid from North Jersey who lives in Brooklyn could come to so fully inhabit and redefine the world of Southern barbecue?) You see this commitment in every bite at Fette Sau; you see it in the steaks and wine at St. Anselm, his Brooklyn steakhouse; you see it in the remarkable craft beer list at his bar, Spuyten Duyvil. Joe doesn't just do his homework in order to make a concept work; he crafts his concepts in order to tell the story he wants to tell. I think it's no coincidence that he got his start like I did—not in the kitchen, but in the music world. This is a man who knows how to connect with an audience.

And yet growing an audience is not what drives Joe Carroll. As it turns out, this isn't just a guy who can write a hit song: He's a guy who decides to write that song not because he thinks it will sell, but simply because the music is in him and because he knows that it is great. And in any industry, such unwavering commitment and unflagging service to a great idea is nothing short of inspiring. As you read this cookbook, I think you'll agree.

INTRODUCTION

AN UNLIKELY PITMASTER

I CANNOT CLAIM any kind of barbecue pedigree. I grew up in New Jersey; my parents hail from the Bronx. We didn't spend our summers crisscrossing the South in search of legendary brisket, ribs, and pulled pork; we spent it in our backyard, cooking dinner on the grill.

We lived on the second floor of our four-family apartment building, so running back and forth to the kitchen was a pain. Instead, I brought the kitchen to our backyard. Starting young helped me become a fearless cook: I rarely used recipes, and I loved to experiment. My approach to cooking has always been "Why not?" I would rather try something that hasn't been done before than replicate a dish from a book. As teenagers, my buddy Brendan and I grilled pizza and lobsters long before it was a thing other people did. While some of my experiments failed, I learned enough from both my successes and my mistakes to have become a confident, decent cook by the time I moved to New York for college.

But I never planned on a career in food. I began my career in the New York City music industry as a consultant to record labels on promotion, sales, and A&R. When my wife, Kim, and I found ourselves without jobs during the dot-com bust of 2002, we moved into my parents' building in New Jersey. Broke and bored, we started visiting garage and estate sales to pass the time, filling a storage locker with secondhand furniture and antiques but not knowing what, if anything, we were going to do with them. One day we saw a gorgeous mahogany bar from the 1920s at a sale for $180; I returned the next day, talked the owner down to $50, and loaded it into my Chevy Astro van. "I guess we have to open a bar now," I said to Kim. So we did.

I've been a beer lover since I was in high school, when I would buy bottles of Guinness Extra Stout (the good stuff, imported from Canada) while my friends drank whatever fizzy yellow beer was the cheapest. During my college years I read everything I could find on beer, mastered the art of home-brewing, hounded beer importers for obscure European beers, and worked a short stint at a beer-focused Belgian restaurant in the East Village. So when we found a location for our bar on a not-yet-gentrified stretch of Metropolitan Avenue in Williamsburg, Brooklyn, I knew exactly what kind of establishment I wanted to open: a little beacon of craft beer in a sea of PBR, where we'd serve brews nobody else carried, the kind of stuff that would make my fellow beer geeks flip out.

We opened Spuyten Duyvil in September 2003 and spent the next three years working our tails off there. The bar was successful beyond our expectations, but Kim and I became restless, and I began thinking about what to do for our next project. Some people start with a concept and find a space to match. I had lots of concepts in mind, so I looked for spaces that could house one of them.

It turns out I'd been staring at it through Spuyten Duyvil's front windows for three years. In the winter of 2006, a neighbor, J. D. Merget, who owns a coffee shop around the corner, told me that the auto-mechanic garage across the street was for rent. I stopped by to take a look: it was as rough and nasty as you would imagine an old garage to be, a truly fucked-up space set back from the sidewalk, its walls seasoned with decades of grease and exhaust. I knew immediately which of my projects would fit into it, the *only* one of my ideas that could work there: a barbecue joint.

Along with beer, I'd had a longtime obsession with smoked meat. It began in 1990 at a restaurant called Brothers Bar-B-Q, a little hole-in-the-wall in Manhattan's West Village, where a guy from North Carolina made pulled pork and ribs and served only vinegar sauce. I was a poor NYU student at the time and Brothers offered something called "Pig-Out Tuesdays," $20 for all you could eat. My first taste of their pulled pork was manna, and it flooded me with memories of the pig roasts my parents' friends threw every summer during my childhood. I remembered getting up at 4 A.M. to help put the pig on the spit and tending the glowing fire all day. After hours over the coals, the pig's crispy skin would shatter like glass in your mouth. We'd pick that carcass clean by the end of dinner. One time my dad's friend cracked the pig's skull open and we ate its brains with a spoon.

After my first trip to Brothers, I was hooked. I loaded my shelves with barbecue books and bought a $40 Weber Bullet smoker that I kept at my parents' house. On the weekends, I'd smoke anything I could get my hands on. I picked up the basic technique pretty quickly but had no real idea of how good my barbecue was, so I started traveling to the big four regions of American barbecue—Texas, Kansas City, Memphis, and the Carolinas—in search of legendary barbecue restaurants and stands; among them, Lexington Barbecue, in North Carolina; Sweatman's BBQ, in South Carolina; Sonny Bryan's Smokehouse, in Dallas; Stubb's, in Austin; Jim Neely's, in Memphis; and Arthur Bryant's and Jack Stack's, in Kansas City.

Early on in my travels, any barbecue in the South seemed awesome, but after a few trips, I figured out that the most famous spots were often not the best; they'd become corporatized, or the pitmaster had left, or the joint had been largely forgotten after national chain restaurants moved into the area. So I started seeking out some lesser-known American barbecue cookery, such as mutton, in western Kentucky; *barbacoa*, in southern Texas; tri-tip, in California's Santa Maria Valley; pit beef, in Maryland; and spiedies and Cornell chicken, in upstate New York. I hadn't come across anything about these micro-regional pockets of what I call "outsider" barbecue in my reading; all my books had focused on the big four regions.

At home (that is, in my parents' backyard), a barbecue style of my own began to take shape. I learned that using meat from sustainably raised, heritage-breed animals resulted in food that was much, much better than anything I'd tasted before, even at those famous temples of 'cue. This was in the days before locavorism and heritage meats had become part of the food conversation; my biggest motivation for using these meats was that they had far more flavor than the commodity stuff from the supermarket. I also developed a preference for the "dry" style of barbecue I'd encountered in North Carolina and especially Texas, where the meat was coated in a dry spice rub (or often just salt and pepper) before a long, hot nap in the smoker. I preferred the way this method develops an intensely flavored crust (or "bark"), as opposed to "wet" barbecue, which is basted as it cooks and coated in sticky-sweet sauce afterward. My approach let the meat speak for itself and relied on wood smoke and patience as its primary ingredients.

By the time I'd signed a lease on the vacant garage, I knew exactly what kind of spot I wanted to open: an amalgamation of the best bits of barbecue culture I'd picked up over the years and a friendly, unpretentious place where meat was king. And I didn't want our barbecue to be handcuffed to any regional style of barbecue. Barbecue is to Americans as beer is to Germans: we're highly suspicious of anything that's not from where we grew up. Any German thinks the best beer comes from his hometown and that everything else is poison. The same goes for barbecue in America: If you grew up in Memphis, you believe that Memphis-style barbecue is the greatest thing in the world and everything else is shit. Texans say barbecue is beef and beef only; North Carolinians swear allegiance to pork alone. Texans think barbecue sauce is blasphemous; Kansas City worships its sticky, shiny glaze; and on and on. My own style of barbecue had become impossible to categorize by this point, having incorporated a cut of meat from one region, a hardwood from that one, and a smoking technique from another, until the result was a mutt of American 'cue filtered through the mind of an Irish-Italian kid from Jersey.

I did not want our place to feel like a typical New York barbecue restaurant. I'd come to consider barbecue a democratizing food that transcends culture, race, and income. This is still true in regions where barbecue has its deepest roots, but elsewhere in America, barbecue has largely become another big-box dining concept. Our strip malls are filled with "BBQ" restaurants that offer gigantic menus filled with cheeseburgers, chicken wings, dozens of sides, and behemoth desserts, and where much of the so-called "barbecue" never sees the inside of a smoker (a fact the restaurants mask with veneers of artificially smoky sauce). And while there was some great barbecue in New York, the vibe at these places didn't match the more down-and-dirty atmosphere I loved about the old-school joints in the South.

So I set out to create the antithesis of what barbecue had become in much of America. My restaurant would operate like the great meat markets of central Texas, which were opened in and around the towns of Lockhart and Taylor by German immigrants in the early twentieth century. These markets operated much like a cafeteria: customers lined up in front of a meat counter stocked with smoked brisket, ribs, and sausages and ordered their meat by the pound from the carver, who piled their orders on butcher paper and sent them off to eat, shoulder to shoulder, at picnic tables. (In many ways, this is the setup of the classic New York delis.)

These markets didn't offer much in the way of sides, mostly crackers and pickles and whatever else could be stocked on the shelves; most of them didn't have separate kitchens for preparing food beyond the barbecue. I planned on keeping with the meat-market theme by offering only a handful of sides: baked beans, my grandmother's cold broccoli salad, and my grandfather's potato salad, plus some locally made pickles and Martin's potato rolls. Mac 'n' cheese and French fries would be forbidden. Hell, I didn't even want to offer utensils: like pizza and hamburgers, barbecue is best eaten with your hands.

The restaurant would serve craft beer, but we would focus on local brews and serve them in growlers and Mason jars. I had also developed an affinity for American whiskey, which we'd serve with big ice cubes or with filtered water measured in eyedroppers.

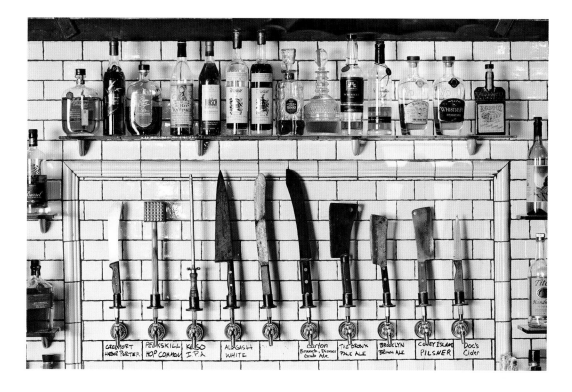

During construction, I almost walked away from the project several times. My fears were many: I wasn't a restaurateur, I was too late to the barbecue craze that was taking over the city, the space was too dilapidated to ever resurrect. I woke up every morning in a panic, but the one thing I was sure of was my barbecue—I knew it was as good as or better than anything I'd tasted anywhere else. That kept me from bailing out.

We named the restaurant Fette Sau. Though its literal translation, "fat pig," connects nicely to barbecue, my wife's German heritage, and barbecue's Germanic roots in central Texas, it actually has a more unflattering and mischievous meaning in German parlance, something Kim and I discovered when we first ran across the phrase in a German drinking song. (This is probably part of the reason so many German tourists now visit the restaurant, and why they always snicker when they see our signs, and why in German television interviews the hosts ask me to say the name of the restaurant.)

We finally opened in March 2007, and there's been a line out the door ever since. If I had opened Fette Sau in Texas, Memphis, Kansas City, or the Carolinas, we would have been called carpetbaggers and run out of town, but in Brooklyn, our customers and the press had fewer ingrained opinions on what proper barbecue should be. Living in a melting pot, New Yorkers are more open-minded about new cuisines and nontraditional cooking. They didn't challenge Fette Sau's half-breed style of barbecue; they embraced it. And while many people who grew up around great barbecue came to my restaurants expecting to hate it, I've had countless folks from one of the big four regions tell me, "This is the best barbecue I've had—outside of my hometown." For me, that's the ultimate compliment.

A couple of years after opening the original Fette Sau, I began to get the itch to build another restaurant. Once again, I didn't have to go far to find the spot. When the space next to Spuyten Duyvil became available, I jumped on it.

We opened St. Anselm in 2010 with a menu of highbrow junk food: deep-fried hot dogs, foie gras pierogi, and the like. It was a doomed conceit from the start: I'd broken my own rule of letting the space dictate the restaurant. So we shut the restaurant down, ripped out the deep fryer, and replaced it with a giant grill. We reopened St. Anselm as a neighborhood restaurant with a heritage meat–centric menu, to waves of positive press. Some folks called it a steakhouse, but I always think of it as a charterhouse of char, where almost every dish touches the grill before it hits the plate. When selecting the meat and seafood we feature at St. Anselm, I thought about what I liked to grill at home. I'm a big fan of underdog proteins like hanger steak, lamb saddle, and head-on prawns; in addition to being less expensive than the more coveted porterhouse, lamb chops, and lobster, they're usually much more flavorful. I inherited a love of charred vegetables from my grandmother, so many of our side dishes also spend some time over the fire.

As with the barbecue at Fette Sau, we want the effects of smoke and fire to be present in every bite, unadulterated by complicated sauces and garnishes.

The funny thing about grilling is that I had never studied it the way I did barbecue; it was just a skill I developed through a lifetime of cooking in my backyard. My approach to grilling is simple and straightforward: if you're not going to put some char on the food, there's no point in firing up the grill. And, as with barbecue, it all begins with selecting great ingredients. A bad piece of meat can't be rescued, no matter how many other ingredients or flourishes you throw at it. But a high-quality heritage-breed steak or chop doesn't need more than some salt and a lot of heat to become the best thing you've ever tasted.

In 2012, I opened a second Fette Sau in Philadelphia's Fishtown neighborhood with restaurateur Stephen Starr. The space is larger than the Williamsburg original, though the look is nearly identical, complete with a barbed-wire fence and antique knives on the beer taps—and the same line of hungry carnivores. I don't see the demand for smoke and char diminishing any time soon, so no doubt there will be more restaurants to come.

Ironically (or inevitably, perhaps), the highly personal, regionally untethered, mongrel style of barbecue restaurant I developed for Fette Sau has itself become something of a regional classification. There are now dozens of joints—maybe more—around the world that model themselves on what's increasingly called "Brooklyn barbecue." The best of these echo the Fette Sau approach by breaking from established barbecue traditions and developing their own style using carefully sourced meat; the worst are just aping a concept, complete with eerily similar butcher-diagram murals, worn knives for tap handles, and Edison bulb–lit flea market décor. Will "Brooklyn barbecue" be a thing fifty years from now? Only time will tell.

In the meantime, I decided to share my live-fire cooking philosophy with you in this book. At first I was hesitant to do so: Why would anyone listen to me? I'm neither a trained chef nor a pitmaster on the competitive barbecue circuit (well, with one exception—which I'll cover later). I'm a self-taught home cook whose most important job is to feed his family and friends. I have no secret recipes or magic touch, but I do have the knowledge amassed by a weekend warrior who has spent a lifetime grilling and smoking in his backyard, and I've trial-and-errored my way into a unique place in the food world. So I thought that the lessons I've learned along the way could help home cooks harness the mighty power of smoke and fire and apply it to pretty much anything they want to cook over a live fire.

HOW TO USE THIS BOOK

THIS BOOK BREAKS my approach to smoking and grilling down into twenty straightforward lessons, with recipes sprinkled throughout to help you apply what you've learned at home. My style of live-fire cooking is pretty simple, but it relies on a real understanding of how smoke, fire, and ingredients interact, as well as on conscientious and informed shopping.

I'm not a gear junkie; I believe amazing food can be cooked on almost any kind of equipment (even indoors) if you know how to build and maintain a fire, are able to get high-quality ingredients, and can master time and temperature. This book will teach you the importance of wood as fuel and the many shapes and forms it can take. And it will show you how great meals begin at the butcher shop and farmers' market.

I think the story of American barbecue—like many histories—has been unfairly dominated by the winners. You've certainly heard of the barbecue of central Texas, Kansas City, Memphis, and the Carolinas. But what about western Kentucky, Santa Maria Valley, or upstate New York? Or even my own home state of New Jersey? All of these areas are home to their own unique styles of barbecue. I have loved discovering these lesser-known pockets of American 'cue, and I take you to them throughout the book to broaden your understanding of our country's signature cuisine, and to help you replicate these distinctive styles of barbecue at home. After all, you may not hail from a bastion of barbecue, but that doesn't mean you can't make big-league barbecue.

Finally, one of best things about live-fire cooking is the sense of celebration that comes with it. Whether you're grilling a batch of burgers or roasting a whole pig on a spit, a party is sure to ensue. And what fun is a party without something to drink? Each of my establishments has its own approach to libations: at Spuyten Duyvil, we focus on fine craft beers; Fette Sau pours locally made brews and America's best whiskeys; and at St. Anselm, we showcase my favorite wine producers from around the world. Each of these categories—beer, whiskey, and wine—is spotlighted in a different chapter, featuring new pairings for barbecue and grilled food, or just as something amazing to drink on its own.

My hope is that whether you want to smoke a better brisket, master whole fish or vegetables on the grill, or experiment with some uncommon barbecue (pulled lamb leg, perhaps?), you'll absorb these live-fire lessons and then adapt them to your own style. Happy cooking!

LESSON NO 1 | MEAT MATTERS

NO MATTER HOW GOOD your equipment, technique, or fuel, you will never achieve barbecue nirvana or a perfectly grilled steak if you don't start with high-quality ingredients. When I began to get serious about barbecue in the 1990s, there wasn't much talk yet about heritage breeds and locally raised animals. But I lived near a great butcher in lower Manhattan, and when I started buying my meat there, I immediately noticed the difference in flavor and texture compared to the meat I had access to growing up in New Jersey.

My real eureka moment happened about a year before we opened Fette Sau, when my chef friend Sara Jenkins invited a few restaurant industry folks over for an informal pork taste-off. She had ordered five pork shoulders: four were different heritage breeds from local farms, and the fifth was a commodity pork shoulder she'd picked up in the supermarket. Even before we started cooking, you could see a sharp contrast between the commodity pork and the others: the heritage pork was fatty and had a deep redness to it, like a piece of great veal; the supermarket pork was lean and gray and smelled like a grocery store. After roasting the shoulders, we could taste subtle differences among the heritage breeds—each had its own unique complexity— but the commodity pork was practically flavorless.

What's more, it's easy to make a case against eating meat from factory-farmed animals. You're eating animals bred to grow as quickly as possible (and often to be leaner and less flavorful); these are animals that have been raised on chemically treated feed in dirty, inhumane conditions. With that commercial meat, you're ingesting potentially harmful drugs and chemicals. And you're eating animals raised with methods that hurt the environment in countless ways. So buying high-quality sustainably raised meat is not just about choosing meat that's far more delicious; it's about not putting crap into your body and not contributing to an industry that is hurting us and the planet.

My simple style of barbecue won't give you the best results if you don't use the best meat you can get your hands on. As I've seen a focus on heritage meats and ingredient-forward cooking take hold of the fine-dining scene, I have been amazed that it hasn't trickled down to the barbecue industry. No matter how perfectly you smoke or grill a piece of protein—or how you dress it up with rubs, sauces, and accompaniments— if you start with a mediocre product, you'll end up with one. On the other hand, a flavorful cut needs very little to become the best piece of meat you've ever tasted.

In order to get the best meat available, you have to ask some questions: Where did the meat come from? How were the animals raised? What were they fed? When

and how was the meat processed, packed, stored, and shipped? To help you answer these, consider the following criteria—listed in descending order of importance— when buying meat.

① NATURALLY RAISED

First and foremost, the meat you cook and eat should be from animals raised without the use of antibiotics, hormones, steroids, or other growth-promoting medicines or chemicals. They should also have been fed an additive-free, 100-percent vegetarian diet. Unfortunately, the USDA's formal definition of "natural" requires only that the meat has been minimally processed, with no preservatives or artificial ingredients added. And that is true of pretty much all fresh meat, rendering the "natural" label meaningless. It leaves room for animals that have been treated with hormones and antibiotics at some point in their lives. So the label alone probably won't tell you if you're buying my definition of "naturally raised" meat; you need to ask your butcher or farmer or do a little research to determine its provenance.

② HERITAGE BREED

Whenever possible, buy meat from heritage breeds. As the industrialization of livestock increased during the twentieth century, we lost hundreds of breeds traditionally raised for meat. They were replaced by commercial breeds favored for growing quickly under large-scale factory farm conditions. This "cheap meat" has dominated our dinner tables and restaurants since the middle of the last century, and only recently have we begun to embrace the difference and value of heritage-breed animals. These animals thrive in open pastures and are more resistant to disease and parasites, making antibiotics less necessary. Plus, a farmer who chooses to raise heritage breeds takes more care with his animals. And the meat

from heritage animals always tastes better than that of their commercial counterparts, as they've been bred for flavor, not productivity. Of course, raising these breeds requires more time, effort, and money than an industrial operation, and the costs are carried over to the customer. But the extra expense is worth it.

③ SMALL FARM–RAISED

There will be large farming operations whose animals meet the previous two criteria, but if you have the option, buy from smaller, family-run farms. First, it's good to support their business: small farms are an ecological asset that promotes biodiversity and sustainable agricultural practices, and they are also a great example and teaching tool for our food industry at large. Without them, we'd all be eating gray pork and bland chicken. I've also found that small-scale farmers treat their animals with an extra degree of care: if nothing else, each animal in a small operation is that much more essential to the bottom line. Generally speaking, the closer you can get to the source of the meat, the easier it is to know that you're buying a great product.

④ LOCALLY RAISED

Barbecue is inherently a local cuisine; there's an obvious reason beef dominates Texas and Kansas City barbecue, pork rules the Carolinas, and lamb is popular in Kentucky. In the New York/ New Jersey area, though, we don't have a strong connection to any specific livestock, so when I can't find a local source for my meat, I order it from all over the place: Colorado (lamb), Iowa (pork), and Texas (beef). You should always favor quality over proximity, but when you can find great meat raised close to home, on local farms, buy it. If you can't find high-quality options anywhere close to where you live, there are many online retailers that specialize in heritage and responsibly raised animals (see Resources, page 255, for some of my favorites).

⑤ ORGANIC

In order for its meat to be labeled "organic" by the USDA, a farm must comply with a strict set of requirements: its animals must be born and raised on certified organic pasture with unrestricted outdoor access, must never receive hormones or antibiotics, and must subsist on a certified organic diet. But getting certified as an organic farm is a time-consuming and expensive process that many smaller operations can't afford—although they can't label their food as such, many of these farms do follow organic practices. So if the meat you buy satisfies all of the other criteria *and* is really organic, consider it a bonus.

HOW TO IDENTIFY GOOD MEAT

It would be wonderful if we could always know the history of every piece of meat we purchase, but reality often leaves us staring into a butcher case or meat aisle full of anonymous protein without a clue about what to choose. To help you make the right choice in those situations, follow this animal-by-animal guide.

Beef

Much of beef's overall quality is determined by breed, how the cow was raised, what it was fed, and when and how it was processed (a more genteel way of saying slaughtered, butchered, and packed, all part of the criteria discussed previously). But fat content is another indication of quality, and it's the easiest to spot with your own two eyes when nothing else of the beef's provenance is known. More marbling—that is, thin striations of intramuscular fat—equals more flavor and tenderness. The USDA helps determine how much marbling is present in a cut of beef by assigning it one of eight grading levels.

The USDA grades you need to know about for the purpose of barbecue and grilling are the three top grades: prime, choice, and select. Select meat contains a slight amount of marbling, and it's what you'll probably encounter at the supermarket. But its low fat content means that select beef is best suited to braising and other wet-cooking methods. Choice beef, which you'll encounter most often at restaurants and butcher shops, has more marbling (about twice as much as select) and is a good option for most grilling and barbecue applications. Prime beef is the best of the beast;

it has the most intramuscular fat and, thus, will be the most tender and flavorful. But prime beef accounts for only about 2 percent of the beef that is graded, and much of it ends up in high-end restaurants.

Keep in mind that not all beef in the United States is graded; while all beef must pass USDA inspection, grading is strictly optional. Much of the meat I buy is ungraded, but I know exactly where it came from and how it was raised—my farmers don't need the USDA to tell me that they produce a superior product. You should also know that any adjectives not preceded by "USDA" that are used to describe beef—"premium," "butcher's choice," "prime selection," and so on—are meaningless marketing terms and should be ignored.

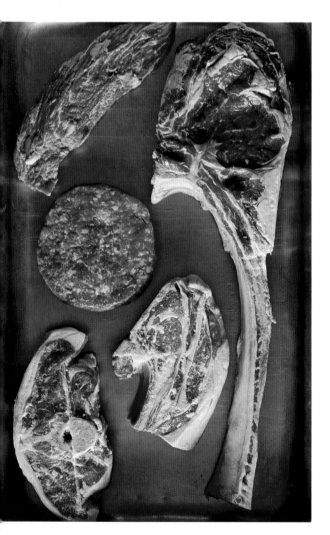

You've probably come across the term "Certified Angus Beef" on menus and in the butcher case. This trademarked brand name means that the beef has met a specific set of criteria and is either prime or (much more likely) choice. It does not mean, however, that the meat came from a pure-breed Angus steer. The Angus breed—which came to the United States by way of Scotland in the nineteenth century—is prized among producers for its marbling and speed of maturation and, as such, is often used for crossbreeding. The defining characteristic USDA inspectors look for is a hide that's at least 51 percent black, which indicates that there are *some* Angus genes in the animal, but they do not conduct genetic testing to verify the exact makeup.

You still have more choices to make when buying beef. While marbling accounts for much of a cut's flavor and tenderness, how (and if) the meat was aged also has an effect. Once it's processed and the muscles have relaxed from rigor mortis, beef can be packaged and sold as "fresh" or further matured through either wet- or dry-aging. "Wet-aged" beef has been vacuum-packed and allowed to mature in a refrigerated environment; it is considered wet-aged because it is in contact with its own blood in its airtight packaging. Most supermarket meat has been wet-aged to some degree. The process will tenderize the meat slightly, but it doesn't have a profound effect on the flavor. Grocery stores prefer this method, however, because there's less moisture loss—and, therefore, little lost weight (and money).

"Dry-aged" beef has been allowed to hang out in contact with the air under tightly controlled conditions for several weeks or longer, which gives enzymes, microbes, and oxygen time to react with the meat and fat. This process changes the flavor of the meat; the longer it's aged, the more concentrated its beefy flavor becomes. Beef that's been dry-aged for an extended period of time will take on a gamey, fermented—some say cheesy or mushroom-like—flavor; how funky you like your meat is a matter of personal preference. During dry-aging, beef can lose up to one-third of its weight through moisture loss, but what it loses in water it gains in flavor (and, ultimately, price). Dry-aged beef is usually available only at butcher shops or the fanciest of supermarkets. If you find you don't like the flavor of dry-aged beef, save your money and buy the freshest meat you can find.

Next comes diet—not yours, the cow's. Most of the high-quality meat in America comes from animals pasture-raised on grass, then fattened on a grain-based diet in feedlots before processing. There's no denying that the meat from "grain-finished" cattle is fattier than that from cows that eat only grass until slaughter. One-hundred-percent grass-fed beef is leaner and, thus, less tender when cooked—especially on the grill or with other high-heat methods. Grass-fed beef is plenty flavorful, though in a different way from grain-finished beef; some people say it's gamey or fishy-tasting, others love the flavor. I prefer meat from a pasture-raised cow finished on grain.

Note that I haven't said anything about color when it comes to choosing beef. Modern processing and packaging technology make it easy for producers to preserve the rosy-red color of fresh meat well beyond its sell-by date. A piece of beef that isn't cherry red isn't something to be afraid of, as long as you're buying it from a source that can tell you enough about the meat to determine its quality.

If you can't find out where your meat came from, how it was raised, or how the USDA has graded its quality, you have to rely on your eyes. Is the meat well streaked with little veins of fat, or is it mostly muscle? If the latter, skip it when grilling or barbecuing and seek out another piece. When all else fails, find a butcher and start asking questions.

Pork

It's much easier to shop for high-quality pork than for good beef. Always choose heritage-breed pork. As far as I'm concerned, there's heritage-breed and then there's everything else. Not only is heritage-breed pork fattier and more flavorful than commercial pork, but it's better for you and the environment as well.

Berkshire, Duroc, Tamworth, Red Wattle, Large Black, Ossabaw, and Mangalitsa are some of the best breeds available, and each of these breeds varies somewhat in texture, fattiness, and flavor. I don't think the specific breed matters all that much: if you're choosing naturally raised noncommercial pork, you're probably going to end up with something great. Note: The USDA doesn't use multiple grading tiers for pork. The only two grades are "Acceptable" and "Utility," and fresh meat in the latter category can't be sold to consumers.

An animal's diet always has an effect on its flavor, but this is especially true of pork. Farmers who care about their pigs will provide them with a diverse diet that combines organic grain-based feed with whatever the pigs can forage and root up in the fields and forests where they're raised. Many heritage-breed producers also feed their pigs tree nuts—most often acorns—which gives the meat a rich, complex flavor. (What makes Spain's *pata negra* pigs so desirable is their endless feast of acorns before harvest.) I'm especially fond of pork that has been raised on "spent" grain left from making beer; the sweetness of the malted grains finds its way into the meat. If you're buying pork directly from a farmer, he will be able to tell you about its diet, as will any good butcher.

Color is also more important with pork than with other red meat. Commercial pork is pale pink at best, while heritage-breed meat ranges from dark pink to dark red. When selecting pork, keep in mind that you want it to look more like the color of beef than that of chicken. Lastly, look at the fat content. This will vary based on the breed and cut, but you want noticeable intramuscular marbling and a smooth, white fat cap.

Lamb

Good news: lamb is even easier to buy than pork or beef. Americans eat far less lamb than other meat, so there's a much smaller commercial market and none of the health and environmental hazards that come along with large-scale production. Most of us will find at most two or three lamb options at the market or butcher shop: American, New Zealand, and (less often) Australian.

Like domestic beef, American lamb is usually grain-finished, which increases marbling and gives it a sweeter, mellower flavor than its southern-hemisphere counterparts. Most of America's large lamb producers are based in Colorado or the Midwest, though you can find small farms that specialize in lamb in many parts of the country, allowing you to buy locally raised meat.

New Zealand lamb is typically smaller than American lamb (New Zealand regulations dictate that lamb destined for meat must be less than one year old; the United States doesn't have any age restrictions). New Zealand lamb is also raised exclusively on grass, giving the meat less marbling and a more intense flavor than that of American lamb. Some people prefer the flavor of New Zealand lamb; others find it gamey.

Australian lamb falls somewhere between the other two. In terms of flavor and fattiness, it's usually closer to New Zealand lamb, but the stock has been crossbred with American lamb to create larger, sometimes fattier animals.

Pricewise, American lamb is the most expensive. Demand for domestic lamb is higher and our sheep industry is dwarfed by New Zealand and Australia's output, which keeps their prices lower. When I'm buying lamb to cook at home, I worry less about its country of origin and more about appearance, reaching for whatever has the size and fat content I want.

Chicken

Because chickens are one of the easiest animals to raise in a natural environment, without drugs, chemically enhanced feed, and so on, "good" chicken is more accessible than any other type of protein at the supermarket. But the bad news is that chicken is tagged with a lot of confusing labels. Knowing what these terms mean (or don't mean) will help you choose the right bird.

NATURAL

As with other meats, "natural" can be a misleading term. It has nothing to do with how the chicken was raised or what it was fed; it only means that, upon slaughter, no artificial ingredients (flavoring, coloring, etc.) were added, so the word doesn't have anything to do with quality. Most of what you'll find at the supermarket counts as natural chicken.

HORMONE-FREE AND RAISED WITHOUT ANTIBIOTICS

Even industrially raised chickens cannot be given hormones, so "hormone-free" is just an empty marketing phrase. "Raised without antibiotics" has slightly more weight—it means that the bird (including in its egg form) was never treated with antibiotics. But there's currently no inspection process to verify this claim, and it also doesn't restrict the use of nonantibiotic medicines and chemicals. Even chickens that have been pumped full of antibiotics are technically "antibiotic-free" (though the term is not allowed on labels) at the time of slaughter, because of a required withdrawal period.

CAGE-FREE

No commercial chicken ever sees the inside of a cage: a bird that lives its entire life in a giant commercial coop is technically "cage-free," so you should ignore this label too.

FREE-RANGE

"Free-range" is another ambiguous term. By law, free-range chickens must be given access to the outdoors, but access in this case may be nothing more than a small door to a fenced-in concrete yard that the chickens never venture into from their giant factory-farm coop. Again, it's a term best ignored.

PASTURED

"Pastured" chickens are free to forage for grass, seeds, insects—whatever they can peck at in an open field. Thanks to their diverse diet, pastured chickens are usually more flavorful, and expensive, than commercial chickens.

ORGANIC

The USDA has created strict guidelines for birds labeled "organic." In this context, the term means that the bird's feed has also been certified organic—that is, the grain it eats has been grown in a chemical- and GMO-free field.

KOSHER AND HALAL

These chickens have been slaughtered by hand according to strict religious guidelines. Anyone concerned with how chickens are slaughtered might seek these out. Kosher chickens are also usually treated with salt, which has a similar effect to brining.

AIR-CHILLED

Most chickens are chilled in pools of cold chlorinated water after slaughter. Air-chilled chickens are hung individually in a cold environment. This reduces the risk of contamination, and it also affects the bird's texture and flavor. Air-chilled chickens aren't plumped with added water, which would dilute their flavor. I (and many other cooks) have found that air-chilling also results in crisper skin.

HERITAGE-BREED

Heritage-breed chickens are still a specialty item, not commonly found even at butcher shops, so you should snatch these up if you see them at your farmers' market or a specialty meat shop. If you can't find a heritage bird, look for an organic one that was air-chilled. Generally speaking, steer clear of any chickens with huge breasts; this is an indicator of a commercial breed favored for output, not flavor, and bad farming practices are sure to be involved.

LESSON NO. 2 | WOOD IS AN INGREDIENT

BARBECUE ISN'T BARBECUE without wood smoke; wood is as much flavor as it is fuel, especially when you're cooking simple barbecue. When your only ingredients other than meat are dry rubs, or just salt and pepper, the type of wood you use can have a profound effect on the taste of the finished product.

I like to impart a good amount of smokiness to my barbecue; I want whoever's eating it to smell and taste the smoke right away. Think of wood like a seasoning in the same way chefs use spices in their cooking. As with spices, you want to use enough to make its presence known, but not so much that it overwhelms the dish.

Whiskey blenders, winemakers, and beer brewers strive to maintain a consistent flavor profile from batch to batch and season to season, resulting in a unique and unmistakable product. Most regional American barbecue styles follow a similar approach, employing one type of wood, or a specific blend of woods, usually determined by whatever grows nearby. Texas brisket gets its intense flavor from mesquite and post oak; the pork barbecue of the Carolinas wouldn't be the same

TYPES OF WOOD AND THEIR FLAVORS

mildest   *moderate*

ALDER: Often used to smoke fish (especially salmon), alder has a delicate and slightly sweet flavor.

ALMOND: Best used for seafood and poultry, almond wood produces a light, nutty-flavored smoke.

APPLE: The most popular of the "mild" woods, apple yields a sweet, fruity smoke flavor. It is most often used for pork and poultry, though it also works well as an all-around wood when you want a more subtle smokiness in your barbecue.

CHERRY: Cherry yields a sweet, fruity flavor; it will also impart a rosy hue to fish and poultry.

GRAPE: If you live in or near wine country, you may be able to source dried grapevines for smoking, which will produce a tart, fruity flavor.

MAPLE: Maple has a lot of wood sugar, so it imparts sweeter flavors and aromas. It's great with poultry or pork barbecue that isn't aggressively seasoned.

SARSAPARILLA: Sarsaparilla is a musky-flavored wood that adds a mild root-beer note to poultry and game.

PECAN: Pecan wood gives off a flavor similar to hickory but is less intense. If you can get it, pecan makes a great all-around cooking wood.

without the flavor of hickory and pecan wood smoke; Santa Maria barbecue is tied to hearty red oak; and so on. At Fette Sau, we use a mix of local hardwoods (mostly red and white oak and maple) to smoke our meat. We try to maintain a consistent blend of wood from day to day; if we suddenly switched over to hickory, for example, our 'cue would taste noticeably different.

CHOOSING WOOD

There are dozens of woods that can be used for barbecue and grilling. While it's true that each type produces its own unique flavor of smoke, the differences between one variety and the next can be subtle, especially when you are using them to smoke large cuts of meat already flavored with a spice rub. It's usually not worth the time and expense to seek out more exotic woods like sarsaparilla or pecan if they aren't readily available where you live.

agressive   *most aggressive*

OAK: The most versatile and widely available cooking wood, oak is dense and burns for a long time, making it ideal for smoking larger cuts of meat. Its flavor is strong but not so overpowering that you can't use it on seafood or poultry. I'll often mix oak with other varieties of wood to create a more complex smoky flavor.

HICKORY: A popular all-around wood that's widely available, hickory has more punch than oak and a slightly nutty flavor. Many prefer hickory for pork and beef, and it can be used sparingly with poultry, in combination with other wood.

BEECH: Like oak, beech burns slowly and evenly with a moderately smoky flavor.

ACACIA: Acacia results in mesquite-like flavors, though much less intense and bitter.

PIMENTO: This exotic wood from Jamaican allspice trees is used for traditional jerk-style barbecue. It imparts a tangy, herbaceous flavor similar to that of its berries.

WALNUT: Walnut's hefty, deeply flavored smoke is best matched with big cuts of beef. It's often used in tandem with other milder woods.

MESQUITE: My feelings on mesquite are best summed up with Livia Soprano's words to her son, Tony, in the series' first episode: "You're using mesquite. That makes the sausage taste peculiar." Although mesquite is popular and widely available, use it with caution: it can impart a pungent, bitter flavor that overpowers any cut of meat, especially when used as the only source of smoke. Even if you love that telltale mesquite flavor, it's best used in small amounts with other woods.

That said, not all wood is meant for cooking. Anything with a high sap content—including pine, cedar, and other coniferous trees—should be avoided, as the sap will impart an unpleasant flavor (plus, some say the smoke from coniferous trees can make you sick). Conventional wisdom says that elm, eucalyptus, and sycamore are also unfit for smoking. Likewise, any green wood—that is, freshly cut wood that hasn't been properly seasoned (dried)—will contain too much moisture and sap, making it burn unevenly and sometimes imparting an unpleasant flavor. Always avoid scrap lumber, which might have been chemically treated or stained, as well as plywood.

The best wood for barbecuing and grilling has been either air-dried or seasoned in a kiln. The cheapest and most readily available wood will be whatever grows near you, but before you order from your local firewood supplier, ask them how their wood has been dried; many can sell you wood seasoned specifically for cooking. It's safe to assume that any wood chips or chunks you purchase by the bag at a retailer have been properly seasoned.

At home, you can experiment with various types of wood until you find one—or a combination of two or more woods—that best matches what you want to barbecue. Some woods are too intense to be used on certain meats, others are too delicate. To get you started, pages 30–31 list some of my favorites, arranged by their flavor from mildest to most assertive.

LOGS, CHUNKS, AND CHIPS

Wood used for barbecuing and grilling ranges from whole logs down to chips to pellets, which are made from pressurized sawdust for use in specialty smokers and grills. Most electric and propane smokers only work with wood chips, while charcoal smokers and grills can use wood in any form. A good rule of thumb is to use wood chunks for longer smoking times (2 or more hours) and chips for shorter ones. When barbecuing a large piece of meat, I typically start with a few large chunks, then replenish the supply one or two pieces at a time to maintain a constant stream of smoke. Although whole logs are usually used only in large commercial smokers, you could keep a log fire burning next to your smoker and feed it with partially burned wood, which will provide both the heat of charcoal and the flavor of wood smoke.

LESSON N⁰ 3 | ONE RUB CONQUERS ALL

EARLY IN MY amateur barbecue days, I experimented with all sorts of dry rubs. I would start with the classic trifecta of salt, pepper, and brown sugar, then add spices and other ingredients. One day I had an idea: I'd read something about how cowboys used to sprinkle coffee grounds on their steaks before grilling them, and I'd tried this on steak in the past. I grew up in an Italian household where espresso was always on hand, so I decided to add some finely ground coffee to a basic rub, along with a few spices I thought would enhance the overall flavor: cumin, cinnamon, and cayenne pepper. I rubbed it on a brisket and threw it in the smoker. The result was an epiphany: the bitter roastiness of the grounds and the malty sweetness of the brown sugar were perfect complementary partners, like milk and sugar are to coffee, and the rub enhanced the flavor of the meat without overpowering it.

I tried the same rub on a variety of animals and cuts and found that it was fantastic on just about everything. So when we opened Fette Sau, I decided to use only one rub to give our barbecue its signature flavor. This one-rub approach is common in many of America's legendary barbecue joints, where a singular (and often top-secret) rub is applied to anything destined for the smoker. In Texas, many pitmasters use only salt and pepper, also known as "Dalmatian rub," on their 'cue. Some spots, like Memphis's famous Charlie Vergos' Rendezvous, also finish their barbecue with a dusting of rub.

FETTE SAU DRY RUB

We use this rub on just about everything that we smoke at the restaurant, but you needn't follow the recipe exactly. Feel free to improvise on the ingredients and amounts, reducing the sugar for a less-sweet bark (crust), increasing the cayenne for a spicier one, and so on.

MAKES ABOUT 4 CUPS

1½ cups packed dark brown sugar

1 cup kosher salt

1 cup ground espresso beans

¼ cup freshly ground black pepper

¼ cup garlic powder

2 tablespoons ground cinnamon

2 tablespoons ground cumin

2 tablespoons cayenne pepper

Combine the sugar, salt, espresso beans, pepper, garlic powder, cinnamon, cumin, and cayenne in a resealable container, cover tightly, and shake well to combine. Store in a cool, dry place. The rub will keep for up to 2 months, at which point the coffee will began to taste stale.

TASSO HAM

Tasso ham is a heavily spiced, heavily smoked cured meat that's a staple in Cajun and Creole dishes—among them, jambalaya and maque choux. Tasso isn't technically a ham, as it's made from pork shoulder, not the hind leg. Tasso isn't usually eaten by itself, but its spicy rub, lightly moistened with honey, would make it an intensely flavorful addition to any charcuterie plate.

PORK SHOULDER

　　This recipe calls for a whole pork shoulder, which will yield 5 small "hams." Unless you're feeding a crowd, you can wrap and freeze the extra hams, or you can cut the recipe down to make only one ham; in that case, ask your butcher to cut you a slab of pork butt about 4 inches thick and 7 inches long (or about 1 pound of meat).

MAKES 5 SMALL HAMS

One 5– to 6–pound boneless Boston butt (pork shoulder roast)

CURE
½ cup kosher salt

1½ teaspoons curing salt (see Note, and Resources, page 255)

½ cup packed dark brown sugar

RUB
½ cup cayenne pepper

½ cup dried sage

¼ cup ancho chile powder

¼ cup smoked paprika

¼ cup dried marjoram

2 tablespoons honey

Wood chunks or soaked wood chips

① Carve the pork shoulder into 5 large slabs, each about 4 inches thick, following the contours of the internal muscles (you shouldn't have to do very much cutting). Trim the slabs of any excess fat.

② In a small bowl, combine the kosher salt, curing salt, and brown sugar. Put the pork on a rimmed baking sheet and rub it all over with the cure (you might not need all of the cure). Wrap the pieces individually in plastic wrap and refrigerate for 12 hours.

③ Preheat a smoker to 225°F or set up a grill for smoking (see page 44 or 47). Unwrap the pork and rinse off the cure. Pat the pork slabs dry and place them on another rimmed baking sheet.

④ In a small bowl, combine the cayenne, sage, chile powder, paprika, marjoram, and honey and stir until combined. Cover the pork with the rub, making sure to pat it into any cracks and crevices in the meat.

⑤ Place the pork in the smoker and smoke, maintaining a smoker temperature of between 225° and 250°F, replenishing the charcoal and wood chunks or chips as needed, until an instant–read thermometer inserted into the center of the meat registers 150°F. Total smoking time will be 2 to 3 hours, depending on the size of the pieces.

⑥ Let the hams cool to room temperature, then slice across the grain as thin as possible. The unsliced hams can be wrapped in plastic and refrigerated for up to 1 week or frozen for up to 2 months.

NOTE

Curing salt, also called pink salt, is salt (sodium chloride) combined with sodium nitrite and/or sodium nitrate. It's used to hinder spoilage in cured meats and sausages. For cured meats that are to be smoked (such as ham, pastrami, and bacon), use what's known as Prague powder #1, which contains sodium chloride and sodium nitrite; see Resources, page 255.

DRY RUBS: MORE BARK, MORE BITE

Most barbecue can be divided into two styles: wet and dry. Wet barbecue is brushed, or "mopped," with sauce throughout the smoking process. Dry barbecue is rubbed with a spice blend and then never sees a drop of sauce until it's on your plate (even then, I think adding sauce to dry barbecue spoils a lot of the fun; see page 110).

There's a lot more wet barbecue than dry in America—Kansas City, Memphis, and the Carolinas all largely employ the wet-rub method—but I'm fully committed to the dry style, which is predominantly used in Texas. Some say that wet barbecue yields juicier meat, but I've never found that to be the case. In addition to being less labor-intensive (you don't have to baste dry-rub meat as it cooks), dry-rub meat has a better "bark"—that dark, chewy, deliciously smoky lacquered crust that forms on the surface of the meat.

Bark is the result of several processes that happen as smoke and heat interact with dry-rubbed meat. As the meat cooks, moisture from both the meat (in the form of water and fat) and the smoke (which contains water vapor) hits the dry rub from either side and turns it wet. Over time, this pasty coating begins to dry out again and undergo the magical Maillard reaction, a chemical process in which amino acids react with reducing sugars to create an array of awesome flavors. Particles from the smoke will also cling to the coating and turn it black (one sign of barbecue that hasn't been hit with enough smoke is a bark that's more brown than black). There are no shortcuts to achieving a great bark on your barbecue; low and slow smoking and a lot of patience are the keys.

CREATING YOUR OWN RUB

The quickest way to create your own signature style of barbecue is to devise your own dry rub. There are few rules for what a rub should or shouldn't contain, but you should start with salt as a foundation. I like kosher salt for its coarser texture; it's easy to overseason with fine sea salt, and iodized table salt tastes bitter and metallic. After salt comes sugar. You can use regular granulated sugar, which will just add sweetness, or raw cane or brown sugar if you want to introduce a molasses flavor into the mix. Then decide if you want your rub to be more salty or more sweet; I usually use a 2:1 ratio of salt to sugar, but you can tip the scale in favor of sugar if you want. Some rubs don't contain any sugar, which is just fine, though you might find that your barbecue really misses that sweet note, especially if you're not eating it with sauce.

NOW IT'S TIME TO PLAY. Add your favorite spices and dried herbs, keeping in mind how they'll interact on the meat. Most folks add black pepper and one or more forms of dried chiles (ancho, cayenne, paprika, and/or pepper flakes or generic "chili powder"), some kind of powdered or granulated allium (garlic, onion), and maybe some ground seeds (cumin, fennel, mustard powder), dried herbs (parsley, sage, oregano, tarragon, thyme), and baking spices (cinnamon, cloves, ginger, allspice, nutmeg). When deciding which flavors to combine, think about how these ingredients play in other dishes. If you like chili powder, cumin, and cinnamon in your chili, you'll probably like them on your barbecue.

AFTER YOU'VE SELECTED YOUR INGREDIENTS, consider their texture. You want a fairly uniform consistency to your rub—this helps the flavors blend together as the rub cooks and forms the bark. Anything in larger pieces (seeds, say, or dried herbs) should be pulverized in a spice grinder or with a mortar and pestle. Any lumps of brown sugar should also be broken up.

MIX YOUR RUB WELL IN A BOWL (or pulse it in a food processor if it contains lots of chunky ingredients and you don't want to grind them individually). Your rub will keep for a month or two in a sealed container, but keep in mind that spices lose their intensity over time.

Your rub is now ready to be put to the test. If you don't want to wait hours to see how it performs on a piece of smoked meat, you can get a preview by frying a spoonful of the rub in a little vegetable oil over low heat until it caramelizes and turns crusty. Let the chunk of rub cool a bit, then taste it: this will give you a sense of how the ingredients play with each other—your blend might be too sweet, salty, or spicy, for instance—but keep in mind that you're missing the all-important flavors of smoke and meat, so this is a rough estimation at best.

To apply the rub, sprinkle a handful over whatever meat you're smoking and pat it onto the surface, making sure to get into any folds or flaps of meat. Repeat until the entire piece of meat has an even coating of rub that will penetrate the meat as it smokes and form a nice, even bark; you don't need to actually rub very hard. Generally speaking, larger cuts (brisket, shoulder, belly, leg, and so on) need a thicker coating. Use a lighter coating with smaller cuts and more delicately flavored meats, such as chicken; too much rub will overpower them.

At this point, your meat is ready to smoke, though you can let the meat sit for a while (up to 12 hours) to allow some of the rub to penetrate the meat. I usually apply the rub when I take the meat out of the refrigerator and let it sit on a wire rack until the rub starts to turn moist. If you want to let the rub penetrate the meat for more than an hour or two, place it on a wire rack on a rimmed baking sheet, cover it loosely with plastic wrap, and refrigerate (wrapping the meat tightly in plastic can cause a lot of the rub to fall off when you unwrap it).

WET RUBS

A wet rub basically starts as a dry rub and is then moistened with some kind of liquid. Oil is the most common addition, but vinegar, mustard, beer, whiskey, soy sauce, and melted butter also make fine bases. Wet rubs have the advantage of adhering better to the meat, and you can add flavors that you can't with a dry rub. However, I find that they don't produce the same kind of dark, rich bark that you can achieve with a dry rub, and so I rarely use a wet rub.

LESSON NO 4 | BARBECUE IS A TECHNIQUE, NOT A RECIPE

MEAT + SMOKE + PATIENCE = BARBECUE. You need only these three things to make the best slow-smoked meat you've ever tasted. I should probably build technique into this equation as well, but, as you'll soon see, barbecue is a relatively simple process once you know where to focus your attention.

You've already been primed on how to choose the best meat, which is by far the most important step in achieving barbecue greatness. And Lesson #2 covered how to select the right wood for whatever you're smoking, so at this point, you're ready to choose your equipment. What style of smoker you select will automatically inform your choice of primary fuel: gas, charcoal, or hardwood logs. In this chapter, I take you through your options and, I hope, convince you that less is more, both in price and the complexity of the equipment.

Once you have your smoker, I'll show you how to set it up for barbecuing, and how to monitor and maintain your 'cue throughout the low-and-slow process. After that, you're ready to choose your first barbecue adventure, from the recipes that begin on page 50.

CHOOSING A SMOKER

Long before I owned a restaurant—and, with it, a top-of-the-line commercial smoker—I taught myself how to barbecue in my backyard with a $40 Brinkmann smoker, which continues to turn out some of the best meat I've ever smoked. You can spend hundreds or even thousands of dollars on a fancy high-end smoker, but all you're paying for is convenience and, perhaps, some badass-looking equipment—but certainly not flavor.

Electric Smokers

An electric smoker is the easiest to use: you plug it in, set the temperature, load your meat, and let the machine do its work; all you have to do is add some wood chips periodically. What you'll end up with is, yes, technically, barbecue, but it's almost impossible to create a thick, flavorful bark in an electric smoker, and you can forget about a smoke ring (see page 57). Simply put, electric smokers don't produce the combustion needed to create the flavor of authentic barbecue.

Propane Smokers

Propane smokers are as easy to use as electric smokers but much more portable. As with a gas grill, there's no charcoal fire to attend to, and you can achieve something close to barbecue flavor. But, as with gas grills, something very important is missing: wood. Read on.

Pellet Smokers

Like electric and gas smokers, pellet smokers offer accurate temperature control and require only minimal babysitting during the smoking process. These grill-like rigs burn small cylinders of compressed sawdust to produce a constant output of smoke. While pellet smokers have their fans and are great for cold-smoking, I've found them to produce less smoke—and therefore less flavor—than even electric and gas smokers.

Charcoal Smokers

Consistent temperature is a convenience, but what's lacking in all of the models mentioned above is charcoal. While fresh wood, whether in the form of chips, pellets, or chunks, adds flavor, carbonized wood—that is, charcoal—is equally essential to achieving maximum barbecue flavor.

Most charcoal smokers fall into one of two categories: offset or bullet-shaped. Offset smokers look like a grill with a small firebox attached to one side. The heat and smoke produced in the firebox flow through the barrel-shaped chamber and out through a chimney. It's easier to build and maintain a fire in this style of smoker, but I've found that they're very inconsistent. It's hard to control the flow of smoke, which tends to float above the meat and exit the chimney before it's done its job. Plus, the side of the chamber near the firebox gets much hotter than the opposite side, so the meat will cook unevenly unless you move it around. There are some great offset smokers on the market, and you'll see professional pitmasters trucking around giant versions of them to barbecue competitions, but these are usually very expensive and/or custom-made.

My favorite type of smoker is the bullet-shaped barrel smoker. Some folks actually fashion these smokers from repurposed barrels, but most store-bought models resemble a kettle grill with a long metal tube fixed between the bowl-shaped bottom and the domed lid. The setup for all of these smokers is basically the same: Charcoal and wood go in a pan on the bottom of the grill and then are added through a small door as needed. A water pan is set above the charcoal and below two or more racks to hold the meat. On top goes the lid, which usually has air vents and a thermometer. The most popular barrel smoker on the market is probably the Weber Smokey Mountain (see Resources, page 255), which comes in three sizes. The cheaper Brinkmann smoker is similar in form and function, but it lacks the Weber's adjustable air vents and has a smaller door, which makes adding charcoal and wood more of a pain. It also has a rather vague temperature gauge on the lid (with "low," "medium," and "hot" zones) in lieu of an actual thermometer. (With any smoker, I recommend using an accurate oven thermometer or instant-read probe thermometer to monitor the temperature until you calibrate the built-in thermometer to your desired cooking range.)

But you don't actually need a dedicated smoker to make proper barbecue. A kettle grill can easily be configured into a smoker and will achieve equally great results once you know how to set one up (see page 47).

My advice: If you're new to barbecue, start with an inexpensive bullet smoker (see Resources, page 255). If you catch the barbecue bug after using it for a while, upgrade to something that suits your particular needs (capacity, speed, convenience, etc.). Just remember that if you opt for convenience over charcoal, you're also leaving out flavor.

SETTING UP AND USING A CHARCOAL SMOKER

If you have a charcoal smoker, congratulations! Your barbecue is going to taste great. Now it's time to start smoking. (See page 48 for step-by-step photos.)

1 Remove any ash and debris if the smoker has been previously used and clean the grates. Any leftover particles or residue will also flavor your meat as they heat up, so you want to start with as clean a smoker as possible.

2 Fill a chimney starter about halfway with hardwood charcoal. Loosely crumple a couple of pieces of newspaper and drizzle or spray them with vegetable oil (this helps the paper burn longer and speeds up the charcoal-lighting process). Stuff the paper into the chimney's lower chamber, place the chimney on the smoker's top

grate, and light it. Let the charcoal burn until the coals are glowing red and coated in gray ash, about 15 minutes. Put on a pair of heavy-duty fireproof gloves and carefully dump about half of the smoldering charcoal into the charcoal container. When I barbecue, I like to have a kettle grill or an extra chimney starter nearby and keep a steady supply of burning charcoal in it to replenish the fire—if you're using pure hardwood charcoal, you can throw a couple of unlit chunks into the smoker at a time, but charcoal briquettes must be lighted beforehand or they'll add nasty flavors to the meat.

③ Line the water pan with aluminum foil (this makes cleanup easier), position it over the coals, and fill it about half full with hot water (if you use cold water, it will take longer for the smoke to heat up). The water pan's primary function is to catch the fat that drips from the meat to prevent flare-ups, but it also acts as insulation that helps reduce temperature fluctuations. Some say the water adds humidity and therefore keeps your meat moister, but I've never noticed a difference.

④ Set the metal grates in place, adding the meat to the grates. If you're not filling up the entire smoker with meat, load it from the top down, as there will be a higher concentration of smoke near the top of the unit. Then put the lid on top. Some experts advocate lighting and assembling your smoker and waiting until it reaches optimum cooking temperature before adding the meat, but all of that assembling, disassembling, and reassembling is a pain in the butt, and I've never had an issue with my single-assembly method.

⑤ If your smoker has air vents in the top or bottom, open them up all the way. You can adjust the vents later to control the temperature.

⑥ Open the smoker door and throw a few tennis ball–size chunks of wood or a handful of wood chips on top of the charcoal. Wood chips should always be soaked in water for at least 15 minutes and drained before use, but there's no need to soak wood chunks in water. If you're using chips, keep a ready supply of them soaking nearby.

⑦ If you have a probe thermometer, insert it through the top air vent to monitor the temperature. (My Brinkmann doesn't have any air vents in the top, so I drilled a hole in it for the thermometer.) The smoker will take about 10 minutes to reach 225°F, which is the optimal temperature for cooking most barbecue. As you get accustomed to your smoker, you'll find yourself needing to check the thermometer less and less.

⑧ You'll notice that the temperature will fluctuate up and down as the wood chunks or chips ignite and the charcoal burns down. These fluctuations are inevitable with a charcoal smoker and are nothing to worry about. Your goal is to maintain a range between 200° and 250°F: As the temperature nears 200°F, add a couple of pieces of charcoal (keep a pair of long tongs handy for opening the hot door and adding the charcoal and wood). If the temperature spikes above 250°F for more than a few minutes, remove a piece or two of charcoal or partially close the bottom vent (and top vent, if necessary) to lower the temperature. If your smoker doesn't have air vents, you can briefly remove the lid until the smoker cools down, though this lets a lot of smoke escape.

⑨ When you notice the supply of smoke dying down, add one or two more wood chunks or another handful of chips to the charcoal container. I think it's more important to keep a constant supply of smoke hitting the meat earlier in the cooking process (see How Often to Add Wood, page 52); when the meat nears doneness, I stop adding wood to the fire—any smoke created in the final cooking stage adds little to the overall flavor.

⑩ If you're smoking big cuts of meat, the barbecue process can take all day. While it's impossible to "set it and forget it" with a charcoal smoker, you don't need to constantly babysit your barbecue. Check the temperature and smoke level every hour or so, and add small amounts of charcoal and wood as needed. As long as your mean temperature is around 225°F, you'll have nothing to worry about.

BARBECUE TIMES AND TEMPERATURES

The chart below gives smoking times and temperatures for the various meats and cuts most commonly used for barbecue. My target smoking temperature for most barbecue is 225°F.

You'll notice that the range of cooking times for any given meat can be quite large; this is because of many small factors, including the temperature of the meat when it begins cooking, the mean temperature of your smoker, the temperature *outside* of your smoker, and even the breed of animal. I've included a target internal temperature for when the meat is done, but that is far less important than the texture of the meat, which you should check first, following the recipe's directions.

MEAT	APPROXIMATE WEIGHT/SIZE	IDEAL SMOKER TEMPERATURE	APPROXIMATE COOKING TIME	INTERNAL TEMPERATURE WHEN DONE
Beef brisket (whole)	10 to 14 pounds	225°F	12 to 16 hours	185° to 195°F
Beef short ribs	7 pounds per rack	225°F	5 to 6 hours	180°F
Beef tongue	2 to 3 pounds each	225°F	6 to 8 hours	175°F
Beef cheeks	1 pound each	225°F	5 to 7 hours	175°F
Pork shoulder (Boston butt)	5 to 8 pounds	225°F	7 to 13 hours (1½ hours per pound)	185° to 195°F
Pork spareribs	3 pounds per rack	225°F	5 to 7 hours	180°F
Pork belly	12 to 15 pounds	225°F	7 to 9 hours	175°F
Pork baby back ribs	1½ pounds per rack	225°F	3 to 5 hours	180°F
Pork loin roast	5 to 6 pounds	300°F	2 to 4 hours	140°F
Fresh sausages	1½ to 2 inches in diameter	225°F	1 to 2 hours	165°F
Lamb shoulder	8 to 10 pounds	225°F	4 to 6 hours	185°F
Lamb spareribs	1½ pounds per rack	225°F	3 to 5 hours	150°F
Goat leg	5 pounds	225°F	5 to 8 hours	150°F
Chicken	4 pounds	225°F	3 to 5 hours	165°F
Turkey	12 to 14 pounds	225°F	6 to 7 hours	165°F

SMOKING IN A KETTLE GRILL

Kettle grills make pretty good smokers. The main disadvantage is that you have to open the cover to add more charcoal and wood or to check your meat, which lets out heat and precious smoke. So, to make sure you do that as infrequently as possible, I recommend using hardwood chunks over wood chips; they take longer to burn down and, thus, will release smoke over a longer time. Otherwise, the process is very similar to using a dedicated smoker.

1 Remove any ash and debris if the smoker has been previously used and clean the grates.

2 Prepare a chimney starter according to the instructions in step 2 on page 44, filling it about halfway with coals. Dump the charcoal into one side of the grill—over the bottom air vent if your grill has one—leaving the other half free of coals. Place a disposable aluminum tray on the other side to use as a drip pan.

3 Place a few hardwood chunks or a foil packet of wood chips (see page 49) over the coals. Add the top grate and put your meat over the drip pan.

Cover the grill, placing the air vents in the lid over the meat. Open both vents about halfway.

4 Smoke the meat, monitoring the smoker temperature on a thermometer inserted through the top vent. If the grill gets too hot, close the top vent and, if necessary, partly close the bottom vent. If using hardwood chunks, add a couple of pieces of unlit hardwood charcoal when the temperature dips down near 200°F. Or, if your wood chip packet stops producing smoke, remove it with tongs and replace it with a fresh packet. If the wood chips ignite, douse the flames with a squirt bottle.

SMOKING IN A GAS GRILL

Gas grills have the advantage of easy temperature control, but you're going to miss out on charcoal flavor. And gas grills tend to be poorly ventilated, which allows a lot of smoke to escape rather than circulate around the meat. Most gas grills have at least two burners; if yours only has one, you won't be able to smoke on it—sorry.

1 If your grill lights from left to right, turn one burner to medium and put the meat on the opposite side of the grill (you don't have to wait for the grill to heat up; and there's no need for a drip pan with a gas setup unless you want to make cleanup easier). Put a wood chip packet (see page 49) under the grate over the lit flame. If your grill lights front to back, light the front burner, place the wood chip packet under the grate over the burner, and put the meat as far back on the grill as possible.

2 Smoke the meat, adjusting the burner to maintain your desired temperature. Replace the wood chip packet whenever it stops smoking; each packet should last 30 to 45 minutes.

SETTING UP A CHARCOAL SMOKER

① Fill a chimney starter halfway with charcoal. Light the charcoal and let it burn until the coals are coated with ash.

② Fill the water pan halfway with warm water.

③ Throw in a few chunks of wood.

④ Set the metal grates in place and add the meat, loading the smoker from the top down.

WOOD CHIP PACKETS

Whenever you're smoking on a grill (charcoal or gas) or when you want to add an extra hit of smoke to whatever you're grilling, throw a foil packet of wood chips onto the coals, or under the grate and over the burner on a gas grill. To make one, pile a couple of handfuls of soaked wood chips on a square of aluminum foil. Top with another square of foil and fold the sides up to form a packet.

Cut several slits in the top of the packet with a paring knife to allow the smoke to escape. Prepare several of these before you light the grill. Each one should last for 30 to 45 minutes before it needs to be replaced, and you can always freeze any extra packets until you're ready to use them; they'll work straight out of the freezer.

PULLED PORK SHOULDER

Pulled pork is a good way to introduce yourself to low-and-slow smoking. Pork shoulder is a far more forgiving cut than brisket; it's well marbled and has plenty of intramuscular fat, as well as a nice fatty layer underneath the skin. It's also not as sensitive to changes in temperature: if your smoker runs hot, you won't risk drying out the pork. The hardest part of making pulled pork is waiting to tear into it.

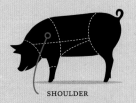

SHOULDER

You can make pulled pork with different pieces of the pig's front and rear legs, but the cut I (and most barbecue enthusiasts) prefer is Boston butt, which is the upper part of the front leg that surrounds the shoulder blade. Some butchers and supermarkets remove the skin and shoulder blade and sell it as "boneless butt," but you want one with both skin and bone intact. The skin helps the shoulder stay moist during cooking, and the bone helps it keep its shape.

When the shoulder is done, you have a decision to make: do you like your pork in large chunks or smaller shreds, finely chopped or thinly sliced? There's no correct answer, and many regional styles of barbecue pork are defined (at least partially) by how the meat is dismantled. I like to actually pull mine into pieces about the size of my thumb. You might want to mix some kind of barbecue sauce into the pork once it's pulled, which is common practice, especially with vinegar-based sauces, in many regional barbecue styles. But I like to leave my pulled pork as naked as possible, maybe seasoning it with a little salt or dry rub, so I can really taste the smoke and the juicy meat (the rewards for my patience).

MAKES 10 TO 12 SERVINGS

One 8-pound bone-in Boston butt (aka pork shoulder roast)

1 cup Fette Sau Dry Rub (page 35), plus (optional) more for seasoning

Kosher salt (optional)

Potato rolls or hamburger buns, for serving

Wood chunks or soaked chips

1 Put the pork shoulder on a rimmed baking sheet and cover it generously with the dry rub, making sure to stuff and pat the rub into any cracks and crevices in the meat. If you have time, let the pork rest for 1 hour at room temperature, or until the rub starts to turn into a pasty coating.

2 Preheat a smoker to 225°F or set up a grill for smoking (see page 44 or 47).

3 Put the pork in the smoker and smoke, maintaining a smoker temperature of between 225° and 250°F, replenishing the charcoal and wood chunks or chips as needed.

continued

4 After about 8 hours, begin checking the pork periodically. When it is done, you should be able to easily pull a hunk of meat off with your fingers; the pork should have a thick, chewy bark and a noticeable pink smoke ring (see The Smoke Ring, page 57) just below the surface. With a towel or thick rubber gloves, grab the bone and give it a wiggle; if it's loose enough to pull from the shoulder, the pork is ready; an instant-read thermometer inserted into the center of the meat should register between 185° and 195°F. Total smoking time can be up to 13 hours.

5 Using heavy rubber gloves, transfer the pork to a rimmed baking sheet. Let it rest for at least 30 minutes.

6 Remove the bone, if you haven't already, and begin pulling the pork into pieces. I find it speeds up the process if you first smash the shoulder a few times with the base of your palm; this will separate it into a few larger pieces, which you can grab and pick apart. As you pull the pork, discard any large pieces of fat that you come across.

7 Once all of the pork is pulled to your liking, taste a piece and, if necessary, season the meat with salt or dry rub. Serve with potato rolls or hamburger buns and sauce on the side, if you like. The pork can be made up to 1 day ahead.

> **NOTE**
>
> To rewarm the pork, put it in a roasting pan or casserole, add a splash of barbecue sauce, vinegar, or water, and cover with a lid or foil. Rewarm in a 250°F oven.

HOW OFTEN TO ADD WOOD

As with any other seasoning, it's possible to use too little or too much wood smoke on your barbecue. I prefer to use more smoke earlier on, keeping a constant supply circulating around the meat for approximately the first half of the cooking time, and then adding wood less frequently or backing off completely toward the end.

I do this for two reasons: Meat absorbs smoke more easily at lower temperatures and by smoking it early in the process, I can guarantee that it will have ample wood smoke flavor. And if you add too much smoke toward the end of cooking, the meat can take on an acrid flavor.

PORK BELLY

You've likely eaten loads of smoked pork belly—it's called bacon. But this pork belly is like nothing you've ever tasted. I've rarely seen fresh, uncured belly smoked like a beef brisket, and when I first tried this, it was incredible: the meat was super-moist and pillowy, and the fat was so soft it actually melted in my mouth. It was so rich and intensely flavorful that I couldn't imagine serving it with barbecue sauce. Why isn't everyone making barbecue belly? I guess they're hung up on bacon.

BELLY

When smoking belly, watch the fat, not the meat, to know when it's done. You should be able to plunge your finger through the fat cap with zero resistance, and the fat should feel like soft gelatin when you rub it between your fingers.

You can also apply this recipe word-for-word to lamb belly, though there's a band of tough connective tissue between lamb belly's layers that you'll want to remove as you slice and serve it.

MAKES 10 TO 12 SERVINGS

1 pork belly (12 to 15 pounds), skin removed

1 cup Fette Sau Dry Rub (page 35)

Wood chunks or soaked wood chips

1 Put the pork belly on a rimmed baking sheet and coat all over with the dry rub, patting it onto the surface until the meat has an even layer of rub (you may not need all of the rub). If you have time, let the pork rest for 1 to 2 hours, or until the rub starts to turn into a pasty coating.

2 Preheat a smoker to 225°F or set up a grill for smoking (see page 44 or 47).

3 Place the belly, fatty side up, in the smoker and smoke, maintaining a smoker temperature of between 210° and 225°F, replenishing the charcoal and wood chunks or chips as needed.

4 After about 6 hours, start checking the meat periodically: Poke the belly in a few places; the fat should be gelatinous and custard-like in consistency, and the meat will easily separate under your finger. If you think the belly is nearly finished, cut off a chunk and eat it. The bark should be dry and crisp, and the meat should be moist and very tender but not mushy. An instant-read thermometer inserted into the center of the belly should register around 175°F. Total smoking time can be up to 9 hours.

5 When the belly is smoked to your liking, use two pairs of tongs or a pair of heavy rubber gloves to transfer it to a cutting board. Let the meat rest for at least 15 minutes, then cut the belly crosswise into ½-inch slices and serve.

NOTE

Barbecue pork belly is best eaten as soon as possible, but if you have to cook it ahead of time, let it cool to room temperature, then wrap it in multiple layers of plastic and refrigerate. To rewarm the belly, unwrap it and place it in a roasting pan. Add a splash of water and cover with foil, then heat it in a 200°F oven until warmed through. If the bark has gone soft, you can recrisp it over a medium–hot grill fire for a few minutes.

THE SMOKE RING

Much has been made of the smoke ring, a band of pinkish meat found directly below the bark in many kinds of barbecue. Some mistake it for undercooked meat, but it's actually the result of a chemical reaction between dissolved smoke gases and meat juice that prevents the meat from turning gray. Others say a thick smoke ring is the sign of great barbecue, but I've never found it to tell me anything other than that the meat was smoked. If your 'cue doesn't have a smoke ring, don't worry: it probably just means you should add more smoke next time.

ROOM-TEMPERATURE MEAT

You've probably read elsewhere that it's important to bring meat up to room temperature before smoking or grilling it, but I haven't found this to have any effect on the final product whatsoever. There's nothing wrong with letting meat warm up before cooking. In fact, I often take meat out of the refrigerator an hour or so before I cook it so I can apply a dry rub or, when grilling, salt the meat ahead of time (see Salting, page 157). But taking meat directly from the fridge to the smoker is just fine; it will just take a little longer to cook.

BARBECUING IN THE COLD

You can barbecue outside all year round, but it gets tricky when the temperature dips (or plummets) below freezing: the cold will make it difficult to maintain an even temperature in your ideal smoking range. So if you want to do cold-weather 'cue, get ready to add fuel more frequently. Smoking meat in cold temperatures takes most of the fun out of barbecue, so I rarely do it, but if you want to brave the elements, you can cloak your smoker in some kind of fireproof insulation, such as a hot-water heater or welding blanket, to keep the temperature up.

ST. LOUIS–STYLE PORK SPARERIBS

When Americans think about barbecue, they probably picture a rack of glistening, burnished pork spareribs. They're the obsession of every competition pitmaster and a menu fixture anywhere barbecue pork is to be found. They also happen to be my favorite ribs to smoke: they're meaty, with a deep, porky flavor and just enough marbling to keep them moist.

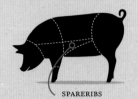

SPARERIBS

Ask your butcher for St. Louis–style ribs, which are spareribs with the rib tips removed. You can also use baby back ribs for this recipe; they're less meaty and will take an hour or two less to cook.

Many sparerib recipes have you remove the membrane from the underside of the ribs before cooking them. I don't see the point, unless you're entering your ribs in a barbecue competition: it's a pain in the ass to remove and there's barely any meat on that side of the ribs, and I also like the extra structure that the membrane gives the rack, which makes it easier to move it around.

MAKES 4 TO 6 SERVINGS

Two 3–pound racks St. Louis–style pork spareribs

1 cup Fette Sau Dry Rub (page 35)

Wood chunks or soaked wood chips

① Put the ribs on a rimmed baking sheet and coat all over with the dry rub, patting it onto the surface until the meat has a thin, even layer of rub (you may not need all of the rub). If you have time, let the meat rest for 1 hour at room temperature, or until the rub starts to turn into a pasty coating.

② Preheat a smoker to 225°F or set up a grill for smoking (see page 44 or 47).

③ Place the racks of ribs, meaty side up, in the smoker and smoke, maintaining a smoker temperature of between 200° and 225°F, replenishing the charcoal and wood chunks or chips as needed.

④ After about 5 hours, start checking the ribs periodically: You should be able to easily tear a piece of meat from the bone with your fingers, but the meat shouldn't be falling-off-the-bone tender. An instant-read thermometer inserted in the center of the rib meat should register about 180°F. Total smoking time can be up to 7 hours.

⑤ Using tongs or a pair of heavy rubber gloves, transfer the racks to a cutting board and let rest for 10 minutes, then cut into individual ribs and serve, with sauce on the side, if you like.

NEW JERSEY BARBECUE

As surprising as it may sound, my home state of New Jersey has a barbecue subculture all its own, one that predates the modern wave of Applebee's-style barbecue chains the state hosts too. While there are plenty of these around the Garden State, there's also a pocket of legitimate barbecue hidden among the heavily wooded Pine Barrens in the southern part of the state. In warmer months, you'll find a smattering of roadside stands here, each spring bringing a new crop of barbecue entrepreneurs.

One of the area's standbys is Uncle Dewey's Outdoor BBQ Pavilion, located along Route 40 in Mizpah (see Resources, page 255). Its proprietor, Dewey Johnson, moved to the state from South Carolina in 1941 and worked as a union representative until retiring and opening his seasonal operation in the lot next to his childhood home. Here, he smokes briskets and pork shoulders in large brick pits, using only salt and local cherry or oak wood to flavor the meat. He also makes chicken and pork ribs, served with a tangy, secret-recipe sauce. Dewey's style of barbecue is clearly influenced by his Southern roots, though it bears little resemblance to the smoked pork of his native state. "A lot of people move up here from the South," he says, "so it makes sense that there's a demand for good barbecue around here."

Nearby is Henri's Hotts (see Resources, page 255), where owner Doug Henri smokes his version of Texas-style barbecue—brisket, pulled pork, ribs, and chicken—in portable smoking rigs behind his restaurant. Like me, Henri claims no regional barbecue heritage: his parents hail from Philadelphia and New Jersey and he grew up an army brat in Germany. "I'm not from the South," he says, "but I know what good Southern barbecue should taste like."

For me, these two spots show that barbecue culture is portable: A small enclave of localized barbecue can spring up anywhere, anytime—even in New Jersey, and probably all over America. All it takes are a few folks who want to fire up a smoker, and enough hungry customers to keep them in business.

PORK LOIN ROAST

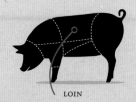

LOIN

A pork loin roast is the porcine version of prime rib, a cut that offers a bit of everything: loin muscle, tenderloin, loin, and baby back ribs. The presence of extra-lean meat warrants extra-careful attention to prevent it from drying out: this is one of the few times that I barbecue meat to temperature—rather than rely on texture—to know when it is done. I smoke the pork at a higher temperature too, which helps keep it moist.

Loin roasts range in size from 5 to 15 pounds, so you can ask your butcher to prepare you a center-cut roast according to your needs: figure one rib per serving. Ask him to crack the chine bone—which attaches the loin to the spine—between the ribs, to make dividing it into chops easier, or have it sawed off entirely. Your butcher might offer to "French" the roast by removing the meat between the ribs. Tell him no thanks, that you're making barbecue and don't want to be robbed of the precious rib meat. If you can only find a boneless loin roast, you can follow the same method; the total cooking time will be slightly less.

MAKES 8 SERVINGS

One 5- to 6-pound center-cut bone-in pork loin roast (8 ribs), chine bone cracked or removed

1 cup Fette Sau Dry Rub (page 35)

Wood chunks or soaked wood chips

① Put the roast on a rimmed baking sheet and coat all over with the dry rub, patting it onto the surface until the meat has an even layer of rub (you may not need all of the rub). If you have time, let the meat rest for 1 hour at room temperature, or until the rub starts to turn into a pasty coating.

② Preheat a smoker to 300°F or set up a grill for smoking (see page 44 or 47).

③ Place the roast, rib side down, in the smoker and smoke, maintaining a smoker temperature of between 250° and 300°F, replenishing the charcoal and wood chunks or chips as needed.

④ After about 2 hours, start checking the meat. The pork is done when an instant-read thermometer inserted into the center of the roast registers 140°F. Total smoking time can be up to 4 hours.

⑤ Using tongs or a pair of heavy rubber gloves, transfer the roast to a cutting board and let rest for 10 minutes before cutting into individual ribs.

BEEF BRISKET

Brisket is the most difficult barbecue to get just right: There is a narrow window between the time when this tough, lean cut turns moist and tender and when it starts to dry out. To make matters worse, brisket comes in various weights and thicknesses and is often divided into two cuts by the butcher: the flat, or first cut, and the point, or second cut (also called the deckle), which is thicker, with a larger fat cap. Ideally you'll buy the biggest, fattiest, highest-grade whole brisket you can find, which will reduce your margin of error. Prime-grade beef will have the most marbling. If you can find only separate first or second cuts, opt for the latter.

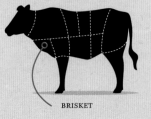

BRISKET

The key to sublime brisket is to turn the meat's connective tissue, which is made up of collagen, into soft, tender gelatin. I like my brisket to have some texture to it—not tough, of course, but pleasantly chewy, like a tender piece of steak. If you smoke brisket too long, it'll turn into stringy, mushy pot roast. Your brisket is done when it's cooked to your liking, and the only way to determine this is to tear off a piece and eat it. When all of your senses go off—the bark is crisp, the meat is toothsome but tender and has that unmistakable flavor of wood smoke—it's ready to be pulled from the smoker.

MAKES 10 TO 12 SERVINGS

1 whole beef brisket (10 to 14 pounds)

1 cup Fette Sau Dry Rub (page 35)

Wood chunks or soaked wood chips

1 Trim the brisket's fat cap to about ¼ inch thick, removing any hard lumps of fat. Put it on a rimmed baking sheet and coat all over with the dry rub, patting it onto the surface until the meat has an even layer of rub (you may not need all of the rub). If you have time, let the meat rest for 1 hour at room temperature, or until the rub starts to turn into a pasty coating.

2 Preheat a smoker to 225°F or set up a grill for smoking (see page 44 or 47).

3 Place the brisket, fatty side up, in the smoker and smoke, maintaining a smoker temperature of between 210° and 225°F, replenishing the charcoal and wood chunks or chips as needed.

4 After about 8 hours, start checking the meat periodically: Poke the brisket in a few places—the fat cap should be soft and pliant and the meat should separate under your finger. If you think your brisket is nearly finished, cut off a chunk and eat it. The bark should be dry and crisp and the meat should be moist and tender but not mushy or overly chewy. An

instant-read thermometer inserted into the center of the brisket should register about 185°F. Total smoking time can be 12 to 16 hours.

⑤ When your brisket is smoked to your liking, using two pairs of tongs or a pair of heavy rubber gloves, transfer it to a cutting board. If your cutting board doesn't have a channel for catching juices, put it on a rimmed baking sheet. Let the meat rest for at least 30 minutes.

⑥ Just before serving (once sliced, brisket dries out quickly), slice the brisket across the grain into ½-inch pieces, beginning at the thinner end of the cut. When you encounter the thick band of tough fat that separates the point from the flat, cut the brisket into two pieces between the point and the flat. Remove most of the fat, then continue slicing and serve.

NOTE

Brisket is best eaten as soon as possible, but if you have to cook it ahead of time, let it cool to room temperature, then wrap it in multiple layers of plastic and refrigerate for up to 1 day. To rewarm the brisket, unwrap it and place it in a roasting pan. Add a splash of water and cover with foil, then heat it in a 200°F oven until warmed through. If the bark has gone soft, you can recrisp it over a medium-hot grill fire for a few minutes.

THE STALL

When barbecuing large cuts of meat like brisket or pork shoulder, you'll notice that the internal temperature rises quickly and constantly over the first few hours of smoking, then stalls somewhere between 150° and 170°F and hangs out there for a few hours before resuming its climb up the ladder. If you're monitoring the temperature of your meat as it cooks (which you don't really need to do), this can be a scary time. Don't worry: the "stall" is caused by moisture evaporating from the surface of the meat, which cools it down until all of the surface moisture has evaporated—the best analogy I've heard is that it's the same as how sweat cools us down on a hot day.

MOVING THE MEAT

Most of the time you can set your meat in the smoker (always fattiest side up) and forget about it until it's finished. There's usually no need to move or turn it unless you notice parts of the cut beginning to burn (this usually happens around the edges)—this is a sign that your smoker has a hot spot. Simply rotate the grate or move the meat.

KNOWING WHEN IT'S DONE

Unless I'm smoking poultry, sausage, or cured meat, I rarely use a thermometer to check doneness when barbecuing (the opposite is true when I'm grilling; see page 170). With barbecue, texture is everything, and a thermometer can't help you with that. Barbecue is a lot like cooking pasta: you have to taste for doneness as it cooks, checking more frequently toward the end.

For beef (brisket, cheeks, and so on), the meat is done when you can easily rip off a piece with your fingers or a fork. Taste it; if it has the right amount of chew, it's done. How tender you like your meat is a matter of personal preference. With ribs, the meat should tear easily when you pull two bones apart.

The texture of the fat is just as important; you want it to feel like soft gelatin—almost liquid—when you poke it with your finger. It shouldn't spring back on you at all.

BEEF SHORT RIBS

Short ribs are the best beef ribs for smoking. They're much meatier than beef back ribs, which are the bones found in prime rib and bone-in rib-eyes and contain very little, and very tough, meat. Short ribs—so named because they come from the "short plate" section of ribs located between the brisket and flank—carry a thick hunk of meat on top of the bone.

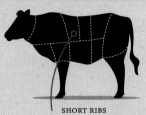

SHORT RIBS

Like brisket, short ribs have lots of connective tissue and need a long, slow spell in the smoker to turn tender enough to eat. And, like brisket, they can be hard to get just right. Short ribs like to trick you into thinking they're done before all of that collagen has melted: the meat on the exterior will be tender before the meat in the center of the ribs—where there's a lot of connective tissue—is ready. To make sure your ribs are tender all the way to the center, dig a little deeper than usual when pulling a piece off to taste it.

MAKES 6 TO 8 SERVINGS

Two 7-pound racks beef short ribs (4 bones per rack)

1 cup Fette Sau Dry Rub (page 35)

Wood chunks or soaked wood chips

① Put the ribs on a rimmed baking sheet and coat all over with the dry rub, patting it onto the surface until the meat has an even layer of rub (you may not need all of the rub). If you have time, let the meat rest at room temperature for 1 hour, or until the rub starts to turn into a pasty coating.

② Preheat a smoker to 225°F or set up a grill for smoking (see page 44 or 47).

③ Put the racks of ribs, bone side down, in the smoker and smoke, maintaining a smoker temperature of between 210° and 225°F, replenishing the charcoal and wood chunks or chips as needed.

④ After about 4 hours, start checking the ribs periodically: You should be able to pull a piece of meat off the bone with your fingers. An instant-read thermometer inserted in the center of the rib meat should register about 180°F, and the meat should be tender all the way through. Total smoking time can be up to 6 hours.

⑤ Using tongs or a pair of heavy rubber gloves, transfer the racks to a cutting board and let rest for 10 minutes before cutting them into individual ribs and serving, with sauce on the side, if desired.

LAMB SPARERIBS

Barbecued lamb ribs are a specialty of Kentucky that doesn't get nearly enough play outside of the state, which is a shame. If you like the flavor of lamb, you'll love lamb spareribs. They're fattier and less meaty than their pork counterparts, but they are smoked in the same manner. You'll notice a lot of external fat on the ribs; some folks have you trim it off before cooking them but, as with any cut I'm smoking, I like to leave all of the external fat on to help keep the meat as moist as possible. You can always remove some of the fat after they're done or, better yet, crisp it up on a hot grill just before serving.

SPARERIBS

MAKES 4 SERVINGS

4 racks lamb spareribs (about 1 ½ pounds per rack)

1 cup Fette Sau Dry Rub (page 35)

Wood chunks or soaked wood chips

① Put the ribs on a rimmed baking sheet and coat all over with the dry rub, patting it onto the surface until the meat has a thin, even layer of rub (you may not need all of the rub). If you have time, let the meat rest for 1 hour, or until the rub starts to turn into a pasty coating.

② Preheat a smoker to 225°F or set up a grill for smoking (see page 44 or 47).

③ Place the racks of ribs, meaty side up, in the smoker and smoke, maintaining a smoker temperature of between 200°F and 225°F, replenishing the charcoal and wood chunks or chips as needed.

④ After about 3 hours, start checking the ribs periodically: You should be able to easily tear a piece of meat off the bone with your fingers, but the meat shouldn't be falling-off-the-bone tender. An instant-read thermometer inserted in the center of the rib meat should register about 150°F. Total smoking time can be up to 5 hours.

⑤ Using tongs or a pair of heavy rubber gloves, transfer the racks to a cutting board and let rest for 10 minutes before cutting them into individual ribs and serving, with sauce on the side, if desired.

PULLED LEG OF GOAT

Although goat is the most widely consumed meat in the world, the demand in America is so low that most goat farmers here—who primarily raise the animals for milk and cheese—either kill male goats at birth or sell them to the commodity meat market. A few years back, Heritage Foods USA (see Resources, page 255) launched their "No Goat Left Behind" program, which promotes the cooking and eating of goats every fall. If you choose to get on board, try my favorite goat-based barbecue.

Many people say that goat is a very gamey meat, but I've always found its flavor to fall somewhere between that of beef and lamb. However, because it contains far less fat than other barbecue-bound animals, you have to pay attention and be sure to take it out of the smoker as soon as it's tender enough to pull, or it can be dry.

LEG

MAKES 8 TO 10 SERVINGS

One 5-pound bone-in goat leg (see Resources, page 255)

1 cup Fette Sau Dry Rub (page 35), plus (optional) more for seasoning

Kosher salt (optional)

Potato rolls or hamburger buns, for serving

Wood chunks or soaked wood chips

> **NOTE**
>
> To rewarm the goat, put it in a roasting pan or casserole, add a splash of barbecue sauce, vinegar, or water, and cover with a lid or foil. Rewarm in a 250°F oven.

1 Put the goat leg on a rimmed baking sheet and generously cover it with the dry rub, making sure to stuff and pat the rub into any cracks and crevices in the meat. If you have time, let the meat rest for 1 hour at room temperature, or until the rub starts to moisten and turn into a pasty coating.

2 Preheat a smoker to 225°F or set up a grill for smoking (see page 44 or 47).

3 Place the goat in the smoker and smoke, maintaining a smoker temperature of between 200° and 225°F, replenishing the charcoal and wood chunks or chips as needed.

4 After about 4 hours, begin checking the goat periodically: When it's done, you should be able to easily pull a hunk of meat off with your fingers and the exterior should have a thick, chewy bark. An instant-read thermometer inserted in the center of the meat should register about 150°F. Total smoking time can be up to 8 hours.

5 Using heavy rubber gloves, transfer the leg to a rimmed baking sheet and let it rest for at least 30 minutes.

6 Begin pulling the goat into pieces. As you pull the meat, discard any large pieces of fat that you come across.

7 Once all the goat is pulled, taste a piece and, if necessary, season the meat with salt or dry rub. Serve with potato rolls or hamburger buns.

SOUTH TEXAS BARBACOA

The history of barbecue is written by the winners. Many of America's hotbeds of modern barbecue share a similar origin story: Some guy—inspired by local cooking traditions, nearby livestock, or pure imagination—smokes a hunk of meat at home, impresses his friends, and is urged to open a barbecue joint. His restaurant/shack/roadside stand is wildly successful, other folks take notice and open similar establishments emulating his barbecue nearby, and, before you know it, a regional style is born.

Sometimes, however, regional barbecue becomes endangered, even extinct. Such is the case with *barbacoa* in south Texas. Though the word has traveled over the centuries from the Caribbean—where it described a wooden contraption used for smoking fish and game—to Europe via Spanish conquistadors and, finally, back to the New World, *barbacoa* in the south Texas tip refers to barbecue made from *cabeza de vaca,* the head of a cow.

Barbacoa was most likely introduced to the region by Mexican ranch hands. Across Mexico, head-based barbecue—be it from a cow, goat, lamb, or pig—has been a weekend-gathering staple for ages. In the cattle ranches near the U.S.–Mexico border, ranch hands, who were often left with the unwanted remnants of livestock butchery, would wrap the heads in maguey (agave plant) leaves and cook them *en pozo*—that is, buried in a pit over smoldering mesquite coals. After a night of steaming and smoking in the earth, the heads would be extracted and unwrapped and the tender meat pulled from the skull and wrapped into tortillas.

The arrival of food-service culture brought with it a proliferation of joints serving *barbacoa* along the U.S.–Mexico border. Over the years, though, modern health regulations have all but quashed the traditional whole-head method; these days you'll still find *barbacoa* on the menu at barbecue joints across Texas, but it's almost always made from beef cheeks or rump roast, often

Today you can find traditional *barbacoa* in exactly one place: Vera's Backyard Bar-B-Que in Brownsville, Texas, located a short stroll away from the Mexican border (see Resources, page 255). Thanks to a grandfather clause, Vera's is the only surviving establishment allowed to serve whole-head barbecue, albeit sans brains, which have been forbidden since the mad cow scare. The restaurant's sign says "Barbacoa en Pozo con Leña de Mezquite," which sums up the cooking method—"barbecue in a hole with mesquite wood"—owner Mando Vera inherited from his father, who opened the restaurant in 1955. Vera wraps the cow heads in foil and buries them in a firebrick pit over mesquite-wood coals. During the slow, 10-hour cooking spell, the head's fat and connective tissue break down, leaving behind impossibly tender, mesquite-scented meat, which is served with tortillas and an assortment of homemade salsas. In addition to being a prime example of barbecue's sweet simplicity, a bite of Vera's *barbacoa* is a taste of history—one that you should experience while you still can.

BEEF CHEEKS

Barbecued beef cheeks are the best part of authentic Texan *barbacoa*, minus the fuss and possible trauma of cooking an entire cow's head.

A cow's cheek does a lot of work (think of all the grass and feed cows eat), making this muscle very flavorful but also extra-tough. A cheek's fat structure is also different from that of most other beef cuts; instead of long striations of marbling, you'll find tiny pockets of fat throughout. For such a tiny cut, the cheeks take a long spell of low-and-slow cooking to get to the right texture, which will be tender but a little chewier than a brisket, like little fists of intensely flavored barbecue. Be sure to save any leftovers for shredding into *barbacoa*-style tacos.

MAKES 4 SERVINGS

4 beef cheeks (about 1 pound each)

1 cup Fette Sau Dry Rub (page 35)

Wood chunks or soaked wood chips

1 Trim any silver skin and large chunks of external fat from the cheeks. Put the cheeks on a rimmed baking sheet and lightly coat them with the dry rub (you may not need all of the rub).

2 Preheat a smoker to 225°F or set up a grill for smoking (see page 44 or 47). Place the cheeks in the smoker and smoke, maintaining a smoker temperature of between 210° and 225°F, replenishing the wood chunks or chips as needed.

3 After 5 hours, start checking the beef cheeks periodically: Pull off a piece and eat it. The bark should be dry and crisp and the meat should be moist and tender but not mushy or overly chewy. An instant-read thermometer inserted in the center of the cheeks should register about 175°F. Total smoking time can be up to 7 hours.

4 To serve, either thinly slice the cheeks and arrange on a platter, or serve one whole cheek per guest.

> **NOTE**
>
> To rewarm the beef cheeks, wrap each in a piece of aluminum foil, adding a splash of water. Heat in a 200°F oven until warmed through. If the bark has gone soft, you can recrisp it over a medium–hot grill fire for a minute or two.

LESSON NO 5 | WHISKEY TAKES TIME

AMERICAN WHISKEY HAS a lot in common with barbecue: both have deep roots in our country's heritage, both are predominantly flavored with charred wood, and both are closely associated with the South. But I don't think whiskey is an ideal partner for barbecue or grilled meat—or any food, for that matter. Whiskey is so assertively flavored and high in alcohol that it will overwhelm almost anything you eat with it. That doesn't mean you can't enjoy a glass of bourbon with your ribs or pulled pork, but you will taste a lot more whiskey than meat. I'd rather have some beer or cider with my barbecue and save my whiskey for afterward. And there's no better way to pass the hours while you're smoking something in the backyard than with a glass of your favorite whiskey—with an ice cube or two on a hot summer afternoon, or with a splash of water during the cooler months.

With wine and beer, I almost always gravitate toward the little guys: small, independent producers who have the freedom to experiment and innovate. With whiskey, the opposite is true. Right now, our country's thirst for American whiskey is higher than ever. This means that established brands can't keep up with the demand and new brands are entering the market at a rapid clip, resulting in price hikes for older brands and an explosion of new microdistilleries across the country—there are even some people making whiskey in Brooklyn. But these upstarts are still in their infancy, and great whiskey takes a lot of time, both to learn the crafts of distilling and whiskey blending and to age it long enough to reap the benefits of years (or decades) of resting in wood barrels.

Many of the new craft whiskey producers are taking chances and creating unique products, but they're also forced to rush their whiskeys to market, which more often than not results in a spirit with a lot of unfulfilled potential. The majority of top-shelf bourbon is matured in barrels for between four and twenty years, but I've seen new distillers age their spirits for only a matter of months. Some are speeding up the process by using smaller barrels or adding oak chips to the whiskey as it ages, but the results are usually disappointing. Others are buying time by bottling white (unaged) whiskey, but supply of those "white dogs" now far outweighs demand. I hope the smaller distilleries can hang around long enough to catch up to the big producers.

A handful of companies owns and operates most of America's best bourbon and rye producers. In other industries (and especially other categories of booze), this could have a negative impact on overall quality, but with whiskey it gives us options at different price points. Can't afford (let alone find) the cultish Pappy Van Winkle bourbon? Seek out the drastically cheaper W. L. Weller, which is made from a

similar mash bill by the same producer (Buffalo Trace). The major difference comes from how and how long the whiskey is aged; the longer it sits in the barrel, the more expensive it gets. Another advantage large distilleries have is the freedom to experiment. Many can release small-batch bottlings of single-barrel whiskeys or play around with various blends from their deep stocks.

WHISKEY PRODUCERS WORTH SEEKING

If you stick to the wares from these four distillers, you will rarely go wrong. Each makes a variety of styles at a wide range of price points, and everything they bottle is at least consistently good to unimaginably great.

Beam, Inc.

Besides the Jim Beam label itself, this portfolio contains some of the first craft bourbons on the market, including Booker's, Baker's, Knob Creek, Basil Hayden's, and Maker's Mark. You'll find at least one of these bottles at pretty much any bar in the country.

Heaven Hill

Kentucky's largest family-owned distillery was founded just after the repeal of Prohibition. It produces a wide range of bourbons, including Cabin Still, Evan Williams, and Elijah Craig, as well as Rittenhouse Rye and Bernheim Straight Wheat Whiskey.

Sazerac

Of the major producers, Sazerac makes the widest range of premium whiskey, most of it out of the Buffalo Trace distillery in Frankfort, Kentucky. Its brands include Ancient Age, Old Taylor, W. L. Weller, Elmer T. Lee, and Buffalo Trace on the younger and less expensive end of the spectrum, and Blanton's, Eagle Rare, George T. Stagg, and Pappy Van Winkle on the long-aged, premium end.

Willett/Kentucky Bourbon Distillers

I've never tasted a whiskey from the smallest of the "big" distilleries that I didn't like. They produce Johnny Drum, Old Bardstown, Pure Kentucky, Noah's Mill, and Rowan's Creek brands, in addition to several bottlings under the Willett name. They also bottle a number of whiskeys under the Kentucky Bourbon Distillers label, including Black Maple Hill, Conecuh Ridge, Michter's, and Old Pogue.

TASTING AND SERVING AMERICAN WHISKEY

When tasting whiskey, look for a balance of aroma and flavor. You won't be able to judge much from color: young and old whiskeys alike can vary in color from light amber to dark caramel. Instead, the first tool to use is your nose: a good whiskey will smell pleasant, with aromas of grains, wood, fruit, and vanilla, and perhaps tobacco and leather as well. A bad whiskey can smell musty or waxy or like raw alcohol.

Most whiskeys aren't meant to be drunk straight; they need a bit of water to cut through the alcohol and open up their great aromas and flavors. If you take a sip of whiskey and it lights up your mouth and throat, you're just tasting the alcohol. Add a few drops of distilled or filtered water (chlorinated water will make it taste like chlorine) and taste again, adding more water until the burn dies down.

After you've taken a couple of sips, think about the whiskey's flavors. With bourbon, you're looking for a balance of sweet corn and the rich vanilla flavors of new American oak. With rye, you want to taste the grain's spicy/peppery/grassy notes integrated with the oak. Any whiskey that tastes like vodka is either too young or was poorly made. This should be true at any proof: a well-made 130-proof whiskey can taste more tame and integrated than a lesser-quality 80-proof one.

From here it comes down to personal preference: Do you like your whiskey more aged or less? Heavy on rye or wheat, or corny as hell? I don't think there's much *bad* American whiskey out there; there's just *better* whiskey. My favorites range from Cabin Still (a remarkably good value for bourbon) up to Willett Rye, which is one of the oldest and rarest ryes on the market.

LESSON NO 6 | KEEP SIDES SIMPLE

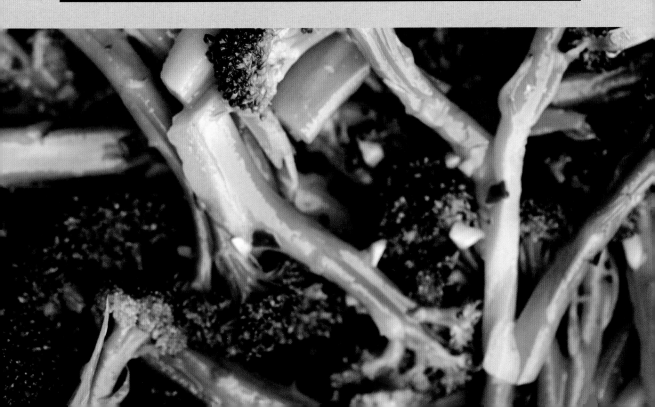

MY BIGGEST BARBECUE inspiration has been the meat markets of central Texas. These barbecue joints began as butcher shops opened by German immigrants, who smoked brisket and sausages in outdoor pits and sold them by the pound. They weren't set up as restaurants with dedicated kitchens, so customers who wanted to eat on the premises would supplement their meals with whatever was being sold on the market's shelves—usually pickles, cheese, bread, and crackers. Even outside of Texas, at the classic barbecue spots of Kansas City, Memphis, and the Carolinas, you don't find a lot of sides on the menu. I love the simplicity of this style of dining, where meat is king. Although I don't have anything against side dishes, when I'm eating barbecue or grilled meat, I like to focus on the protein, and there's only so much you can eat in one sitting.

But I know that people do like to round out their meals. When selecting appetizers or sides, pair barbecue with dishes that are high in acidity, which helps balance the richness of the meat. It's also smart to contrast hot barbecue with cold or room-temperature sides (such as my grandmother's broccoli salad, opposite, or my mom's coleslaw, page 93), especially during hot summer months.

There's an obvious convenience that comes from cooking your sides on the grill. As I mentioned earlier, when I was growing up, my family's kitchen was up two flights of stairs from the backyard, so we'd cook our entire meal on the grill. I've also used my smoker as an oven to bake beans, potatoes, or whatever will benefit from some time in the smoke chamber. When you've already got the heat (or smoke), why not use it?

CORA'S BROCCOLI SALAD

My grandmother's broccoli salad was a staple of my childhood. It's meant to be eaten at room temperature or cold, and its flavors actually improve after a day or two in the refrigerator, which gives the acidic vinaigrette enough time to soak into the crisp broccoli.

MAKES 4 SERVINGS

1 large bunch broccoli (about 1 pound), cut into 1-inch florets, woody stems discarded

2 tablespoons fresh lemon juice

1 large garlic clove, finely chopped

Pinch of red pepper flakes

¼ cup extra-virgin olive oil

Kosher salt and freshly ground black pepper

1 Place a steamer basket in a large saucepan, add 1 inch of water, and bring the water to a boil. Add the broccoli, cover, and steam until crisp-tender, about 5 minutes. Transfer the broccoli to a bowl and let cool.

2 While the broccoli cools, make the vinaigrette: In a small bowl, whisk together the lemon juice, garlic, and red pepper flakes. Slowly whisk in the olive oil. Season to taste with salt and pepper.

3 Toss the broccoli with the vinaigrette and serve immediately, or cover and refrigerate until ready to serve. The salad can be refrigerated for up to 2 days.

DANTE'S POTATO SALAD

This potato salad was a staple at my grandparents' house. In the summertime, my grandfather Dante would make a batch of it every week. It's certainly in the style of German potato salad, but he added olive oil as a nod to his Italian roots. My version of the recipe, with the addition of grainy mustard, nudges it back toward Germany.

MAKES 8 TO 10 SERVINGS

½ cup plus 1 tablespoon extra-virgin olive oil

1 large Spanish onion, diced

4 pounds Yukon Gold or other waxy potatoes

Kosher salt and freshly ground black pepper

2 tablespoons whole-grain mustard

¼ cup cider vinegar

¼ teaspoon cayenne pepper

2 tablespoons chopped chives

① In a large skillet, heat 1 tablespoon of the olive oil over medium-low heat. Add the onion and cook, stirring frequently, until translucent and crisp-tender (you don't want the onion to be completely soft), about 8 minutes; if the onion begins to brown, lower the heat. Transfer to a bowl and let cool.

② In a large saucepan, cover the potatoes with water by 1 inch and add a large pinch of salt. Bring the water to a boil, reduce the heat to a simmer, and cook until the potatoes are tender, about 25 minutes. Drain the potatoes and transfer to a cutting board.

③ Meanwhile, in a bowl, whisk together the mustard, vinegar, and cayenne. Slowly whisk in the remaining ½ cup olive oil. Season the vinaigrette to taste with salt and pepper.

④ When the potatoes are cool enough to handle, cut into ½-inch dice.

⑤ In a bowl, toss the warm potatoes and reserved onions with the vinaigrette. Add the chives, season with salt and pepper, and toss again. The potato salad can be served immediately or refrigerated for up to 1 day.

BAKED BEANS WITH BURNT ENDS

Burnt ends are the trimmings left over from smoked brisket. Traditionally they were considered scraps not worthy of selling to customers, so they were given away or used in beans or stews. But barbecue lovers came to recognize burnt ends for what they are—densely flavored, intensely smoky nuggets of bark—and they became a delicacy. Today, at many barbecue joints, especially in Kansas City, you can order a plate of burnt ends, which are often made from the brisket's fattier second cut (or point) specifically for this purpose.

At Fette Sau, we don't just add burnt ends to our beans: any leftover scraps from the carving station—pulled pork, barbecue belly, ribs, whatever—go into the beans. I recommend doing the same. The more kinds of meat you add to the pot, the richer and more complex your beans will be. If you have especially fatty chunks of meat, stir them in earlier in the cooking process to allow the fat to melt and enrich the beans.

MAKES 8 SERVINGS

1 pound great northern beans, picked over

4 cups water

1 small Spanish onion, thinly sliced

2 large garlic cloves, finely chopped

3 cups Heinz ketchup

½ cup brown ale or other malty beer

¼ cup Worcestershire sauce

½ cup packed dark brown sugar

2 tablespoons Colman's mustard powder (see Note)

1 tablespoon kosher salt

1 tablespoon freshly ground black pepper

½ teaspoon cayenne pepper

1 bay leaf

1 pound brisket burnt ends or assorted barbecue, diced (about 3 cups)

1 Put the beans in a medium bowl and cover with water by 2 inches. Soak for at least 8 hours at room temperature.

2 Preheat the oven to 250°F.

3 Drain the beans and put in a Dutch oven or other large pot. Add all remaining ingredients, except for any leaner pieces of meat, and bring to a boil. Cover the pot, transfer to the oven, and bake for 2 hours.

4 Uncover the pot and stir in any remaining meat. Return to the oven and bake for 2 hours longer. Remove the bay leaf and serve the beans. Or let cool and refrigerate for up to 2 days.

BAKED BEAN-STUFFED ONIONS

I've always been fascinated by chuck wagons and cowboy cooking: I can't imagine a better scenario for dinner than an expansive prairie, a setting sun, and a live fire with steaks and kettles of beans cooking over it. At one point, I even started looking for a vintage wagon, which I wanted to set up in a vacant lot where we'd cook open-fire dinners with a live bluegrass band. (Various New York City departments didn't share my enthusiasm.)

I first made this recipe during my early cowboy phase, around the time I started getting into old country and bluegrass music. Not only does cooking beans inside an onion make for a cool presentation, but the onions add flavor to the beans and vice versa, especially when slowly simmered over a smoky fire. Sweet Vidalia onions make the best onion bowls; they're wide and squat, so they won't roll around on the grill, and they're mild and sweet enough to eat with a knife and fork when you've finished your beans.

MAKES 4 SERVINGS

4 large Vidalia onions, peeled

Olive oil

Kosher salt

2 cups Baked Beans with Burnt Ends (page 86)

¼ cup packed dark brown sugar

① Prepare a two-stage fire with medium and low sides in a grill (see page 149).

② Trim away a little of the root end of each onion so they have a stable base to stand on. Using a paring knife, cut a circle in the top of each one with the knife angled inward to remove a cone-shaped piece of onion. Use a teaspoon to scoop out and discard most of the insides of the onion, leaving about a ½-inch shell. Rub the insides and outsides of the onions with olive oil and season the insides with salt.

③ Fill the onions with the baked beans. Sprinkle the brown sugar over the top.

④ Place the onions over the low side of the grill, cover the grill, and cook until the onions are tender throughout, about 20 minutes. Serve.

GRILLED FINGERLING POTATOES

This simple side dish can be served alongside any meat or other main course you're throwing on the grill. A hot grill crisps up the exterior of the fingerlings so they are like fat steak fries, making them the perfect starch accompaniment.

MAKES 4 SERVINGS

1 pound fingerling potatoes, scrubbed

Kosher salt

Extra-virgin olive oil

Freshly ground black pepper

¼ cup melted Garlic Butter (page 177)

¼ cup chopped parsley

1 Put the potatoes in a large saucepan and add enough water to cover by 2 inches. Add 1 tablespoon salt and bring to a boil over high heat. Reduce the heat to medium and simmer until the potatoes are just tender, about 10 minutes. Drain and let cool slightly, then cut lengthwise in half.

2 Prepare a hot single-level fire in a grill (see page 149).

3 In a large bowl, toss the potatoes with olive oil until well coated. Season with salt and pepper and toss again. Grill the potatoes, cut side down, until charred on the first side, 2 to 3 minutes. Turn the potatoes over and grill until the skin is crispy, about 2 minutes longer.

4 Transfer the potatoes to a bowl and toss with the garlic butter. Season to taste with salt and pepper, sprinkle with the parsley, and toss again. Transfer to a serving bowl and serve.

COLLARD GREENS

I've always thought of collard greens as more of a soul food staple than a barbecue side dish, but I love them with smoked meat. The liquid left from cooking the greens—and you really need to cook them into submission to get them tender enough to eat—is what's known as pot liquor (or "potlikker"), a vinegary, porky broth that's magical in and of itself. Save any leftover potlikker to use in soups or gravies—some Southerners even drink it straight as a tonic.

MAKES 4 TO 6 SERVINGS

2 large bunches collard greens (about 3 pounds)

4 slices thick-cut bacon, cut into 1-inch pieces

2 garlic cloves, finely chopped

1 smoked ham hock, rinsed

8 cups water

One 12-ounce bottle pilsner beer

¼ cup cider vinegar, or more to taste

2 tablespoons dark brown sugar

1 bay leaf

Small pinch of red pepper flakes

¼ teaspoon yellow mustard seeds

1 tablespoon kosher salt, or more to taste

1 teaspoon freshly ground black pepper

1 Cut or tear the woody stems and ribs from the collard greens, and discard any leaves that are bruised or yellow. Wash and drain the leaves (you don't have to dry them well). Stack a few leaves at a time and roll them up like a cigar, then cut crosswise into ½-inch-wide strips.

2 In a stockpot, cook the bacon over medium-low heat until some of the fat has rendered, about 8 minutes. Add the garlic and cook, stirring, for 2 minutes.

3 Add the ham hock, water, beer, cider vinegar, brown sugar, bay leaf, red pepper flakes, mustard seeds, salt, and pepper to the pot, then add the collard greens, packing them down until they're submerged in the liquid. Bring the liquid to a boil, then lower the heat to a simmer, cover the pot, leaving a crack for steam to escape, and cook, stirring occasionally, until the collards are very tender, at least 2 hours.

4 Remove and discard the bay leaf (if you can find it). Remove the ham hock from the greens and, when it is cool enough to handle, remove the skin and pull the meat from the bone. Coarsely chop the meat and return it to the pot.

5 Season the greens to taste with more salt and/or vinegar, if necessary. Serve, or let cool and refrigerate for up to 1 day.

SUSAN'S DILLY COLESLAW

My mom, Susan, makes this fresh, tangy slaw for all of our family barbecues. Her recipe is extremely simple—just mayonnaise, a touch of vinegar, and lots of dill—but you can treat it as a foundation and add other cabbages or vegetables as you see fit.

MAKES 8 SERVINGS

1 cup mayonnaise

1 tablespoon distilled white vinegar

½ cup chopped dill fronds

Kosher salt and freshly ground black pepper

2 pounds white or Napa cabbage (about ½ large head), cored and cut into ¼-inch-wide ribbons

1 In a small bowl, whisk together the mayonnaise and vinegar. Stir in the dill and season the dressing to taste with salt and pepper.

2 In a salad bowl, toss the cabbage with the dressing. Refrigerate for at least 1 hour before serving. The slaw can be refrigerated for up to 1 day.

CHARRED LONG BEANS

A speckling of blistered flesh on vegetables adds both caramelized and smoky flavors, which is so much more interesting than anything a steaming basket can achieve. Chinese long beans, aka yard-long beans, look and taste like gangly, protracted green beans. They're especially grill-friendly, as their length and curly shape will prevent them from slipping through the grates. They make an easy, extra-quick side dish that you can cook in the time it takes for meat to rest after it comes off the grill.

MAKES 4 SERVINGS

1 pound Chinese long beans, trimmed

2 tablespoons extra-virgin olive oil

Kosher salt and freshly ground black pepper

3 tablespoons melted Garlic Butter (page 177)

¼ cup chopped parsley

1 Prepare a medium-hot single-level fire in a grill (see page 149).

2 Bring a large pot of salted water to a boil. Prepare an ice bath. Blanch the beans for 1 minute, then transfer to the ice bath. When they are cool, drain the beans.

3 Put the beans on a rimmed baking sheet, drizzle with the olive oil, and toss until coated, then season with salt and pepper.

4 Grill the beans, moving and turning them frequently with tongs, until crisp-tender and charred in spots, about 3 minutes.

5 Transfer the beans to a serving bowl and drizzle with the warm garlic butter. Sprinkle with the parsley and season to taste with salt and pepper. Toss and serve.

GRILLED HALLOUMI WITH LONG BEANS AND PEA SHOOTS

There are only a few cheeses that can stand up to the heat of a grill without melting through the grates. Of these, salty halloumi is the best. When grilled, this feta–like fresh Cypriot cheese takes on a flavor that reminds us why we love fried cheese. To lighten things up, here I pair it with a springy salad of pea shoots and charred long beans dressed in a lemony vinaigrette, though I've also been known to just grill up a platter of the cheese, dress it with good olive oil and pepper, and snack away. Pea shoots are available in the spring at many farmers' markets, but you can substitute mizuna or frisée if necessary.

MAKES 4 APPETIZER SERVINGS

8 ounces halloumi cheese (available at Greek or Mediterranean markets), cut crosswise into eight ½–inch slices (3–by–½–by– 5–inch pieces)

2 tablespoons extra–virgin olive oil, plus more for brushing

Freshly ground black pepper

1 tablespoon fresh lemon juice

Kosher salt

1 cup Charred Long Beans (page 94), cut into 1–inch pieces

1 cup pea shoots

1 tablespoon finely chopped mixed parsley, chives, and tarragon

1 Prepare a medium–hot single–level fire in a grill (see page 149).

2 Brush the cheese slices with olive oil and season with pepper. Grill the cheese, turning once with a spatula, until charred on both sides and warmed through, 2 to 4 minutes. Transfer the cheese to four plates.

3 In a small bowl, whisk together the 2 tablespoons oil and the lemon juice. Season to taste with salt. Put the long beans, pea shoots, and herbs in a medium bowl and toss with the vinaigrette to taste.

4 Top each plate of cheese with a mound of beans and serve.

CHARRED BROCCOLI WITH PECORINO AND LEMON

I was raised on the flavor of charred vegetables. My grandmother loved to cook vegetables in a blazing-hot skillet until they were almost blackened and took on a meaty, deeply caramelized flavor. This is the grilled version of one of her recipes. Make sure to coat the broccoli all over with oil; this will help distribute heat and lead to even charring. You can also make the recipe with smaller broccoli florets in a grill basket.

MAKES 4 SERVINGS

1 large head broccoli (about 1 pound)

3 tablespoons extra-virgin olive oil, plus more for drizzling

Kosher salt

¼ cup finely grated Pecorino-Romano cheese

Finely grated zest of 1 lemon

Flaky sea salt, such as Maldon

1 Prepare a medium-hot single-level fire in a grill (see page 149).

2 Trim about 2 inches off the end of the broccoli stalk and cut the broccoli into 8 long spears. In a bowl, toss the broccoli with the olive oil until well coated, then season lightly with kosher salt.

3 Grill the broccoli spears, turning them every couple of minutes, until charred all over and crisp-tender, about 8 minutes.

4 Transfer the broccoli to a platter and drizzle with olive oil. Sprinkle with the cheese, lemon zest, and flaky salt and serve immediately.

ICEBERG WEDGE WITH WARM BACON DRESSING AND BLUE CHEESE

Several of the dishes we serve at St. Anselm are small tweaks on classic steakhouse fare. Before it was edged out of fashion, the iceberg wedge was ubiquitous on menus (and dinner tables) in the 1950s and '60s. Instead of the usual buttermilk dressing, I contrast the crisp lettuce with a warm bacon dressing inspired by the jars of gravy-like Pennsylvania Dutch bacon dressing my family poured over salads, vegetables, and potatoes when I was a kid. This salad is one of my favorite accompaniments to a simple grilled steak.

MAKES 4 SERVINGS

BACON DRESSING

6 ounces thick-cut bacon, cut into ½-inch pieces

2 tablespoons all-purpose flour

1½ cups water

⅓ cup cider vinegar

1 tablespoon sugar

1 tablespoon Dijon mustard

Kosher salt and freshly ground black pepper

SALAD

1 large head iceberg lettuce, cut and cored into 4 wedges

4 ounces blue cheese, preferably Cashel, crumbled

¼ cup chopped parsley

1 Cook the bacon in a large skillet over medium heat until crisp, about 10 minutes. Using a slotted spoon, transfer the bacon to paper towels to drain. Pour the bacon fat into a measuring cup and then return ¼ cup of the fat to the skillet.

2 Heat the bacon fat over medium-low heat, then stir in the flour and cook, stirring with a wooden spoon, until the flour is lightly browned, about 2 minutes. Add the water, vinegar, sugar, and mustard, bring to a simmer, and cook, whisking frequently, until the dressing is thick enough to coat the back of a spoon, about 10 minutes. Season to taste with salt and pepper and remove from the heat. (The dressing should have the consistency of gravy.)

3 Put the iceberg wedges on four plates. Drizzle with the warm bacon dressing and sprinkle with the reserved bacon, the blue cheese, and parsley. Serve immediately.

TOMATO AND BURRATA SALAD

Essentially a grilled Caprese salad, this is a great starter or side dish to make when you're already firing up the grill for dinner. Instead of the traditional mozzarella, use burrata, a mozzarella pouch filled with *ritagli* (leftover mozzarella curds) and heavy cream, which ooze out of the silky shell when you tear it apart. This buttery cheese pairs well with the sweet caramelized flavor you get from charring tomatoes over a hot fire.

The beefsteak tomato was destined for the grill: even when perfectly ripe, it's sturdy enough to withstand the heat of the fire. Don't try making this salad with a super-ripe heirloom tomato, or you'll find yourself scraping tomato paste off your grill grate.

MAKES 2 SERVINGS

1 large beefsteak tomato (about 12 ounces)

1 tablespoon extra-virgin olive oil, plus more for drizzling

Kosher salt and freshly ground black pepper

4 or 5 large basil leaves

One 8-ounce ball burrata cheese (available at specialty cheese shops and Italian markets)

High-quality balsamic vinegar, for drizzling

Flaky sea salt, such as Maldon

1 Prepare a hot single-level fire in a grill (see page 149), making sure to oil the grate well.

2 Cut the tomato crosswise in half and brush the cut sides with olive oil. Grill the tomato, cut side down, undisturbed, until charred, 2 to 3 minutes (your goal is to just char the surface of the tomato; you don't want to cook the inside). Remove from the grill and season with kosher salt and pepper.

3 Stack the basil leaves and roll them up like a cigar, then slice into thin ribbons.

4 Place the burrata on a small platter and tear it in half to release the creamy curds. Arrange the grilled tomato halves on either side of the cheese and sprinkle with the basil. Drizzle the salad with olive oil and vinegar, sprinkle with flaky salt, and serve.

CHARRED CORN WITH COMPOUND CREAM CHEESE

There are plenty of grilled corn recipes that call for a compound butter that's spread over the warm corn. Using a compound cream cheese is a similar concept, but the cheese adds a bit of tang and it sticks to the ears better than butter. Here I flavor the cream cheese with za'atar, a Middle Eastern spice blend made from sesame seeds, sumac, and other spices and dried herbs. It's nutty and herby, with a distinct tartness from the sumac.

When it comes to grilling corn, I like mine extra-charred, to the point where most of the kernels have turned dark brown and taken on a smoked nutty flavor—some blackened kernels are fine as well. Otherwise, what's the point of grilling it?

MAKES 8 SERVINGS

4 ounces cream cheese, at room temperature

1 tablespoon za'atar (see Resources, page 255), plus more for sprinkling

½ teaspoon finely grated lemon zest

1 tablespoon fresh lemon juice

Kosher salt and freshly ground black pepper

8 ears corn, shucked

Olive oil, for brushing

1 Prepare a hot single-level fire in a grill (see page 149).

2 In a small bowl, combine the cream cheese, za'atar, lemon zest, and lemon juice and mix with a fork until smooth. Season to taste with salt and pepper.

3 Brush the corn all over with olive oil and grill, turning every minute or so, until blistered and charred all over, 8 to 10 minutes.

4 Transfer the corn to a platter and use a butter knife to spread the cream cheese all over it. Sprinkle with za'atar and serve.

BABY EGGPLANTS WITH FRIED GOAT CHEESE AND CARAMELIZED ONIONS

Eggplants are meant for live–fire cooking. Their flesh soaks up smoke and caramelizes nicely, becoming as meaty in texture as a vegetable can be. Use baby eggplants—their skin is still thin enough to eat and their seeds have yet to turn bitter. You could use large mature eggplants in this recipe, but in that case, peel them first.

MAKES 4 TO 6 APPETIZER SERVINGS

2 tablespoons olive oil, plus more for brushing

1 medium onion, halved and thinly sliced

1 bay leaf

Kosher salt and freshly ground black pepper

2 tablespoons dry white wine

Vegetable oil for deep–frying

¼ cup all-purpose flour

1 large egg

½ cup panko crumbs, finely crushed with your hands

4 ounces Montrachet or other fresh goat cheese, cut into 4 slices and kept cold

Ground coriander, preferably freshly ground

2 pounds assorted baby eggplants, cut into ½-inch slices

Honey, for drizzling

1 Make the caramelized onions: In a large skillet, heat the olive oil over medium heat. Add the onions and bay leaf, sprinkle with salt and pepper, cover, and cook, stirring occasionally, until the onions are softened and golden, about 15 minutes.

2 Uncover the skillet and add the wine. Bring to a simmer, scraping up any browned bits on the bottom of the pan, and cook until the liquid has evaporated, about 2 minutes. Season the onions to taste with salt and pepper and keep warm over very low heat. Remove the bay leaf before using.

3 Fry the cheese: In a medium saucepan, heat 2 inches of vegetable oil to 350°F. Put the flour on a small plate. Beat the egg in a shallow bowl. Put the panko on another small plate. Dredge the goat cheese in the flour and pat off any excess. Sprinkle all over with coriander, salt, and pepper, dip the cheese in the egg, turning to coat, and then coat with panko. Fry the goat cheese until golden brown, about 1 minute. Transfer to a wire rack to cool.

4 Prepare a medium–hot single–level fire in a grill (see page 149). Brush the eggplant slices with olive oil and season with salt and pepper. Grill the eggplant slices, turning once, until tender, 2 to 3 minutes per side.

5 Arrange the eggplant and goat cheese on a platter. Scatter the caramelized onions on top. Drizzle with honey, sprinkle with coriander, and serve.

SANTA MARIA-STYLE TRI-TIP

Like Texas *barbacoa* (page 71), the style of barbecue popular along California's central coast is rooted in cattle culture. In the nineteenth century, ranchers celebrated a successful roundup or marathon branding session with an all-day, Spanish-style feast. The vaqueros dug large pits, filled them with logs of red oak, and cooked various cuts of beef over the flames, serving them with tortillas, salsa, and beans.

But while traditional *barbacoa* has all but vanished in Texas, Santa Maria–style barbecue continues to thrive in the region along California's central coast between San Luis Obispo and Santa Barbara. Today, most of the area's barbecue is slowly cooked on an adjustable grill that can be raised and lowered over a fire, though the choice of fuel has remained the same; many say the mild, sweet smoke of the shrubby red oak tree (aka coastal live oak) gives Santa Maria barbecue its distinctive flavor—a hint of local *terroir*, if you will—and makes it difficult to replicate outside of the region.

Although Santa Maria barbecue encompasses multiple cuts of beef (top sirloin is a favorite), the one most famously linked with the style is the tri-tip, an inexpensive, isosceles-shaped piece from the bottom sirloin that was usually delegated to ground beef or stew meat. It was in the early 1950s that a one-armed butcher named Bob Schutz rubbed one with salt, pepper, and garlic powder and spit-roasted it over a live fire.

Soon, local restaurants like Jocko's, the Hitching Post, and the Far Western Tavern (see Resources, page 255) were serving their own Santa Maria–style barbecue platters, which traditionally include pinquito beans and tomato salsa—both nods to the region's Spanish and Mexican heritage—and garlic bread. Barbecue sauce, it should be noted, is usually nowhere to be seen. These restaurants are still thriving today, as are dozens of other joints that serve Santa Maria–style barbecue, but if you find yourself in town on a Friday night, stop by the Santa Maria Elks Lodge for the weekly CYO (cook your own) dinner, a long-standing local tradition.

Some will argue that Santa Maria "barbecue" is actually grilling, because the meat is not cooked in an enclosed environment. But to me it has all the markers of barbecue: slow cooking over wood smoke. And there are plenty of folks along the central coast who will back me up on that.

SANTA MARIA-STYLE TRI-TIP

The tri-tip is the *tensor fasciae latae* muscle, a triangular cut from the bottom sirloin, which is located near the cow's hindquarters and just in front of the round. If your butcher doesn't know what tri-tip is, ask for this muscle. The meat is fairly chewy and not especially fatty, so it's best thinly sliced across the grain. In California, it's traditionally served with pinquito beans and tomato salsa. The leftover meat also makes for excellent sandwiches.

MAKES 4 SERVINGS

1 tablespoon kosher salt	Pinquito Beans (recipe follows)
1½ teaspoons freshly ground black pepper	Tomato Salsa (recipe follows)
½ teaspoon garlic powder	
1 beef tri-tip roast (about 2 pounds)	½ cup soaked oak chunks or oak chips

① In a small bowl, combine the salt, pepper, and garlic powder and mix well. Generously season the meat all over with this mixture and let sit at room temperature for 1 hour.

② Prepare a two-stage grill with high and medium-low sides (see page 149). Prepare a wood chip packet with oak chips (see page 49) or use two chunks of hardwood.

③ Place the meat over the hot side of the fire and sear, turning once, until well charred on both sides, about 3 minutes per side.

④ Place the wood chip packet or wood chunks over the coals on the medium-low side of the grill (or under the grate and over the burner on a gas grill). Continue grilling the tri-tip, turning it every 10 minutes or so (listen to the meat to know if your grill is the right temperature—you should be able to hear the meat gently sizzle), until it reaches the desired doneness. Timing will be 30 to 35 minutes for medium-rare; an instant-read thermometer inserted in the center of the meat should register 125°F. Transfer the meat to a cutting board and let rest for 10 minutes.

⑤ Slice the meat ¼ inch thick against the grain and transfer to a platter. Pour any accumulated juices over the top. Serve with the beans and salsa.

continued

PINQUITO BEANS

These "little pink" beans are exclusively grown in the Santa Maria Valley, which makes them a natural (and almost inseparable) accompaniment for tri-tip. They stay firm when cooked and are equally good warm or at room temperature. But they're difficult to find outside of California, so you can substitute pinto or other small pink beans.

MAKES 8 SERVINGS

1 pound dried pinquito beans (see Resources, page 255) or pinto beans, picked over

4 cups water

4 ounces slab bacon, cut into ¼-inch cubes

1 red onion, chopped

3 garlic cloves, finely chopped

2 tablespoons dark brown sugar

2 teaspoons Colman's mustard powder (see Note, page 87)

2 teaspoons kosher salt, or more to taste

Hot sauce

2 tablespoons chopped cilantro

① Put the beans in a bowl and cover with cold water by 2 inches. Let soak for at least 8 hours at room temperature.

② Drain the beans, transfer to a medium saucepan, and add the 4 cups water. Bring to a boil, then reduce to a simmer, cover, and cook until the beans are tender, 30 minutes to 1 hour (depending on the beans and soaking time). Turn off the heat, uncover the pan, and let the beans cool in their liquid.

③ In a Dutch oven or other large pot, cook the bacon over medium heat until golden brown, about 5 minutes. Add the onion and cook, stirring occasionally, until softened, about 4 minutes. Add the garlic and cook for 2 minutes longer, then stir in the brown sugar, dry mustard, and salt.

④ Drain the beans in a sieve set over a bowl, reserving the cooking liquid. Add the beans and 2 cups of the cooking liquid to the pot, bring to a low simmer, and cook, stirring frequently, for 30 minutes.

⑤ Season the beans with salt if necessary and hot sauce to taste and garnish with the cilantro. Serve warm or at room temperature. Or let cool and refrigerate for up to 3 days.

TOMATO SALSA

In a nod to the area's Mexican heritage, Santa Maria tri-tip is typically served with a tomato salsa. My version is about as simple as salsa gets, but if you want to add a layer of smoky flavor to the recipe, you can cut the tomatoes and/or onion into ½-inch slices and quickly sear them over a hot grill before chopping.

MAKES 4 SERVINGS

1 pound ripe tomatoes, halved, seeded, and cut into ½-inch pieces

½ small white or red onion, finely chopped

1 jalapeño pepper, seeded and finely chopped

1 tablespoon fresh lime juice

Kosher salt and freshly ground black pepper

Combine the tomatoes, onion, jalapeño pepper, and lime juice in a nonreactive container and season to taste with salt and pepper. Let sit for at least 30 minutes before using. The salsa can be prepared up to 1 day ahead and refrigerated.

LESSON Nº 7 | SAUCE?
IF YOU MUST . . .

MY LESS-IS-MORE APPROACH to barbecue extends to sauce as well. I think that good barbecue should be able to stand on its own. I don't usually like sauce with *any* meat except for ketchup with hamburgers, and I really hate it when my barbecue comes coated in a heavy, sticky varnish. The sad thing about barbecue sauce is that the sauce has become the *definition* of barbecue for many people, who think that slathering a piece of meat with a shiny red condiment turns it into barbecue. This couldn't be farther from the truth. Too much great barbecue is ruined by being drowned in sauce before being served—just as so much truly awful barbecue attempts to hide itself in a bath of the stuff.

That said, I know that many people love barbecue sauce and won't eat barbecue without it. I originally wanted Fette Sau to be a sauce-free barbecue joint, but I was talked into serving it by wiser minds (my wife, Kim). So we came up with three styles of sauce: a sweet tomato-based barbecue sauce, a spicy sauce made with pureed chile peppers, and a vinegar sauce made with cider. These sauces can be used interchangeably with any style of 'cue, though most folks pair the sweet and spicy sauces (or a combination thereof) with smoked beef and poultry and the vinegar sauce with pork.

My personal preferences aside, sauce is one of the few ways you can put your personal stamp on your 'cue. It's also the defining characteristic of many regional barbecue styles, each sauce having evolved to complement its smoked counterpart. In eastern North Carolina, smoked hogs are served with a simple, tangy dressing of vinegar and red pepper flakes, while in the western part of the state, especially around Lexington, a touch of tomato is added to the vinegary base for its pulled and chopped pork shoulders. South Carolina's "mustard belt" takes its name from the intense mustard sauce used to dress its pork barbecue. The funky Worcestershire-based "dip" of western Kentucky is a natural pairing for the region's mutton barbecue. Memphis serves its famous ribs both dry and wet, the latter doused with a thin tomato and vinegar sauce. Kansas City 'cue is usually paired with a thick, sweet tomato sauce, and the legendary Alabama joint Big Bob Gibson's popularized a ranch dressing–like sauce that now pervades the state.

SWEET BARBECUE SAUCE

A sweet molassesy tomato-based sauce is what comes to mind when most people think of barbecue. This type of sauce—which is essentially gussied-up ketchup—was born in Kansas City and has become the inspiration for countless commercial sauces, most notably KC Masterpiece. My version has an equal balance of sweet, savory, and acid. The Worcestershire sauce goes a long way in taming the sweetness of the ketchup, and the beer, cider, and vinegar add enough zip to tie everything together. The trick is to simmer these ingredients for a long time; you want the sauce to turn from crimson into a deep mahogany color as the sugars caramelize. To make the sauce even better, stir in any meat juices you can gather from what you've cooked on the grill or in the smoker.

MAKES ABOUT 2 CUPS

2 cups ketchup

3 tablespoons Worcestershire sauce

2 tablespoons cider vinegar

2 tablespoons hard cider

2 tablespoons pilsner beer

2 tablespoons dark brown sugar

2 teaspoons Colman's mustard powder (see Note, page 87)

½ teaspoon garlic powder

½ teaspoon cayenne pepper

1 teaspoon kosher salt

1 In a large nonreactive saucepan, combine all the ingredients, bring to a simmer, and cook, whisking occasionally, for 45 minutes. The sauce will thicken and darken as it cooks.

2 Let cool. Transfer the sauce to a container, cover, and refrigerate until ready to use. The sauce can be refrigerated for up to 1 month (but if you add meat juices, discard it after a couple of days).

VINEGAR SAUCE

When coming up with a vinegar sauce for Fette Sau, I didn't want something that was too obviously connected to any specific regional barbecue. (North Carolina 'cue employs a sauce that's either vinegar and spices, in the eastern part of the state, or the same with the addition of tomato, in the west; South Carolina adds mustard to its vinegar sauce.) And I wanted a vinegar sauce that would work equally well with all kinds of smoked meat—not just the pork it's usually paired with. This sauce will add brightness to pulled pork, and it has enough depth to stand up to beef and lamb.

MAKES ABOUT 2½ CUPS

2 cups cider vinegar

½ cup Worcestershire sauce

2 tablespoons dark brown sugar

1 tablespoon hard cider

1½ teaspoons kosher salt

1½ teaspoons Colman's mustard powder (see Note, page 87)

⅛ teaspoon cayenne pepper

⅛ teaspoon garlic powder

⅛ teaspoon granulated onion

1 In a large nonreactive saucepan, combine all the ingredients and bring to a boil, then turn off the heat and let cool to room temperature.

2 Transfer the sauce to a container, cover, and refrigerate until ready to use. The sauce can be refrigerated for up to 1 week.

MAKING BOTTLED SAUCE BETTER

As you'll see in these recipes, a decent barbecue sauce doesn't take long to make. But unlike chicken stock or marinara, homemade sauce isn't always better. There are a surprising number of bottled sauces out there that I'd be happy eating (if I loved barbecue sauce to begin with). And there's no harm in tweaking a store-bought sauce: you can play with acidity and heat by adding vinegar and hot sauce or add some savory depth with Worcestershire sauce or drippings left over from the meat.

SPICY CHILE PEPPER SAUCE

Warning: this sauce—which is basically pureed chiles, seeds and all—lives up to its name. But it's not a simple, one-note hot sauce; the combination of three chiles gives it a great depth of rich, smoky flavor. Though folks who love a lot of heat with their 'cue use this sauce straight, I often combine it in equal parts with our Sweet Barbecue Sauce (page 111), which results in the perfect balance of sweet and spicy.

MAKES ABOUT 2 CUPS

2 ounces dried pasilla chiles (about 7 chiles), stemmed

2 ounces chipotle chiles (about 20 chiles)

½ ounce dried chiles de árbol (about 30 chiles)

2 garlic cloves, smashed and peeled

1 small yellow onion, thinly sliced

8 cups water

1 teaspoon kosher salt

1 teaspoon garlic powder

1 teaspoon ground cumin

2 teaspoons cider vinegar

1 In a large saucepan, combine the chiles, garlic, onion, and water and bring to a boil, then lower the heat and simmer, uncovered, for 1 hour.

2 Strain the cooking liquid into a bowl and transfer the contents of the strainer to a blender. Add 1 cup of the reserved cooking liquid, the salt, garlic powder, cumin, and vinegar and blend on high speed until pureed.

3 Pass the chile puree through a fine-mesh strainer into a bowl, pressing on the solids. The sauce should be the consistency of ketchup; add a splash of water if it's too thick. Let cool.

4 Transfer the sauce to a container, cover, and refrigerate until ready to use. The sauce can be refrigerated for up to 4 days.

SPICY MUSTARD

This simple homemade mustard began as something Fette Sau's cooks made for themselves to eat with our pastrami, brisket, and smoked beef tongue. Eventually our customers found out about it and started asking for it. You should know that this is definitely not a French-style mustard sauce. It's most akin to hot Chinese mustard, which is also made from mustard powder. Make sure you use Colman's mustard powder here; the generic powder sold in the spice section is too weak.

You'll find that this mustard is especially pungent at first, but the flavor mellows over time. We've made it with all sorts of beer over the years, so each batch is a little different, depending on the brew. Feel free to experiment with your favorite beers: anything that's not very hoppy should work well.

MAKES A SCANT 2 CUPS

One 12-ounce bottle lager or ale

One 4-ounce container Colman's mustard powder

Pour the beer into a large jar and let the foam settle. Add the mustard powder, seal the jar, and shake well. The sauce will keep indefinitely in the refrigerator, though the flavor will mellow over time.

WESTERN KENTUCKY AND MUTTON

The hog heaven that is Carolina barbecue can be traced back to a surfeit of pork, as can Texas *barbacoa* and Santa Maria barbecue to an excess of ranch steer. And it's no surprise that the meatpacking hub of Kansas City produced one of the country's best barbecue regions. Such is the case, too, with western Kentucky. This part of the Bluegrass State produces a surplus of lamb—and with it, the country's biggest center of lamb-based barbecue.

To be more specific, the sheep that put Kentucky on the barbecue map is mutton, the term used for the meat from older sheep. In the nineteenth century, the state's wool industry boomed, leaving the area's Welsh settlers with a surplus of older sheep whose meat was tough and gamey, and the only way to turn this mature meat into something delicious was a lot of low-and-slow cooking. Barbecued mutton became a fixture at Catholic church fund-raisers and, over the generations, established itself as the region's signature cuisine.

Today the Kentucky wool industry isn't what it used to be, but there's still plenty of mutton to go around. The epicenter of mutton-based barbecue is the town of Owensboro, where two restaurants dominate the scene. The century-old Old Hickory Bar-B-Que (see Resources, page 255) is one of them. There, pitmaster Gary Sandefur watches over the cinder-block smokehouse, the walls of which are coated in a sticky, molasses-colored patina formed by constant plumes of hickory smoke belched out by two giant pits. Inside these iron beasts are dozens of mutton shoulders and legs, which get bihourly mops of black "cooking dip" during the 22-hour-long smoking process required to break them down into something palatable.

But the mutton that comes out of Old Hickory's smokers is more than palatable: It has considerable bark and plenty of fat, with a telltale musky flavor that is best tamed by the region's tart, Worcestershire-based sauce. You can have it sliced, chopped, or on the rib, with the option of paying 50 cents per order extra for meat served straight "off the pit," which is worth the modest splurge.

An even larger operation resides a couple of miles away at the Moonlite Bar-B-Que Inn (see Resources, page 255), which the Bosley family has operated since

1965. Today, owner Ken Bosley and four of his children (plus their families) run the business, which goes through some 10,000 pounds of mutton each week while feeding a 350-seat dining room as well as a takeout counter and catering business. While hickory-smoked chicken, beef, and pork share the menu with mutton, the latter still dominates diners' plates. Moonlite also specializes in another local specialty: burgoo, a spicy, homey stew made with—what else?—mutton.

But Kentucky has more to offer to barbecue culture than mutton alone. Head further west from Owensboro and you'll find lots of chopped or pulled pork, served with a spectrum of sauces that seem to vary by the county. And in the southeastern part of the state, Monroe County and its surrounding areas offer a unique pork-based specialty I've not encountered outside of the region. Here, frozen pork shoulders are sawed into thin slices, bone and all, then grilled over a hickory fire while being basted with a spicy vinegar-based sauce. Good specimens of "shoulder," as the locals call it, can be found at spots like Frances' Bar-B-Que in Tompkinsville (see Resources, page 255). Owner David Arms recently reopened the establishment his mother, Frances, built in 1977, after the original structure burned to the ground. He credits his dad for the restaurant's spicy vinegar-based sauce, which he says comes from a 150-year-old recipe given to him "by a 110-year-old black man."

A few miles away in Gamaliel, Collins Barbecue (see Resources, page 255) also serves a proper sliced shoulder, cooked over scrap hickory on a makeshift pit behind a cinder-block bunker. There, the aptly named young owner, Jay Dee Wood, swears he's neither heard of nor tasted mutton, even though Owensboro is two hours up the road. "Mutton? What's that . . . goat?"

I'm hesitant to even classify Monroe County shoulder as barbecue, as the meat is cooked fairly quickly over an open flame, but don't tell the folks down there. To me, this is evidence that Kentucky is the perfect microcosm of American barbecue culture. People just a few counties apart are cooking distinctly different styles of 'cue, each stubbornly believing that theirs is the one and only thing, just like Carolinians view barbecue through porcine-tinted lenses while Texans believe that true barbecue can only be made with beef, and so on. Everyone's right—and nobody's right—at the same time.

PULLED LAMB SHOULDER

Lamb and pork shoulder are structurally similar: both have lots of intramuscular fat and connective tissue that, after a long afternoon in the smoker, break down into tender, easily pulled meat. You could make this recipe with a bone-in leg of lamb as well, but a leg will have less fat and is more expensive.

For true Kentucky-style flavor, use hickory wood for smoking and serve the lamb with the Owensboro Worcestershire Sauce.

MAKES 10 TO 12 SERVINGS

1 bone-in lamb shoulder (8 to 10 pounds)	Potato rolls or hamburger buns, for serving
1 cup Fette Sau Dry Rub (page 35), plus (optional) more for seasoning	Owensboro Worcestershire Sauce (recipe follows)
Kosher salt (optional)	Wood chunks or soaked wood chips

① Place the lamb on a rimmed baking sheet and generously cover it with the dry rub, making sure to stuff and pat the rub into any cracks and crevices in the meat. If you have time, let the lamb rest for 1 hour at room temperature, or until the rub starts to turn into a pasty coating.

② Preheat a smoker to 225°F or set up a grill for smoking (see page 44 or 47).

③ Place the lamb in the smoker and smoke, maintaining a smoker temperature of between 225° and 250°F, replenishing the wood chunks or chips as needed.

④ After about 4 hours, begin checking the lamb periodically: You should be able to easily pull a hunk of meat off with your fingers and the lamb should have a thick, chewy bark. An instant-read thermometer inserted in the center should register about 185°F. Total smoking time can be up to 6 hours.

⑤ Using heavy rubber gloves, transfer the lamb to a rimmed baking sheet. Let it rest for at least 30 minutes.

⑥ Begin pulling the lamb into pieces. As you pull the lamb, discard any large pieces of fat that you come across.

⑦ Once all of the lamb is pulled, taste a piece and, if necessary, season the meat with salt or dry rub. Serve with potato rolls or hamburger buns and the Owensboro Worcestershire Sauce.

NOTE

To rewarm the lamb, put it in a roasting pan or casserole, add a splash of barbecue sauce, vinegar, or other liquid and cover with a lid or foil. Rewarm in a 250°F oven.

continued

OWENSBORO WORCESTERSHIRE SAUCE

The predominant flavor in this traditional mutton accompaniment is Worcestershire sauce, the centuries-old condiment made from a base of vinegar-fermented anchovies, which lends it its telltale umami-rich flavor. In western Kentucky, this funky sauce is a natural pairing for the region's gamey lamb barbecue.

MAKES ABOUT 3 CUPS

1½ cups water

½ cup Worcestershire sauce

½ cup stout or porter

½ cup distilled white vinegar

1 tablespoon ketchup

2 teaspoons fresh lemon juice

3 tablespoons dark brown sugar

1 teaspoon kosher salt

½ teaspoon freshly ground black pepper

¼ teaspoon ground allspice

¼ teaspoon onion powder

¼ teaspoon garlic powder

① In a medium nonreactive saucepan, combine all the ingredients, bring to a boil, and cook until slightly reduced, about 5 minutes. Let cool.

② Transfer the sauce to a container and refrigerate. The sauce can be refrigerated for up to 1 week.

THERE ARE TIMES when barbecuing outdoors isn't an option, due to weather or to lack of time, equipment, or location (e.g., a city apartment). While you can't really barbecue meat (fish is another story; see the recipe on page 125) indoors, you can infuse almost anything with the flavor of wood smoke by buying a stovetop smoker or fashioning your own. If I'm craving some barbecue chicken in the dead of winter, say, I'll roast a whole bird in the oven, then finish it in a stovetop smoker for 15 minutes or so. The same works for ribs, pork shoulder, and any other meat you typically associate with barbecue.

Stovetop smoking also opens up new flavor possibilities: in addition to wood chips, you can use most of the spices in your kitchen or loose-leaf tea to infuse the meat. While the smoky flavor won't infuse as deeply as a long spell in a dedicated smoker, it's the closest you can get to real 'cue in the comfort of your own kitchen.

SETUP

There are several decent stovetop smokers on the market. Camerons makes the most popular of these; it looks like a roasting pan with a tight-fitting lid and it costs around $50.

If you don't want yet another piece of equipment clogging up your kitchen, you can easily fashion your own smoker using a baking pan or a deep wok. Place the aromatics (see below) on the bottom of the pan and set a wire baking rack on top. Arrange the food on top of the rack and set the pan over medium heat. When the first wisps of smoke appear, cover the pan tightly with a lid or aluminum foil. If your stove has an exhaust fan, you should definitely turn it on, though there's no way to prevent your kitchen from smelling at least a little like a smokehouse (which can be quite pleasant).

Aromatics

Choose aromatics for stovetop smoking as you would spices for a dry rub, blending ingredients based on your personal preferences and the flavor profile you want to infuse into the food. Wood chips will offer up the same flavors as chunks and logs (see pages 30–31 for a wood selection guide), and smoking with tea evokes Asian cuisine. I often use a combination of both chips and tea, along with some dried spices and herbs.

Wood Chips

Use the smallest wood chips you can find; they will smolder more readily than larger pieces. Always soak the chips for 30 minutes beforehand, and then wrap them in a foil packet according to the directions on page 49 (if burned directly on the surface of the pan, they can scorch and stain your cookware). Wood pellets, designed for pellet smokers and grills, are also great for stovetop smoking, and they don't need to be soaked.

Tea

Tea-smoking is common in certain Asian cuisines. You can use any fragrant tea; I like jasmine tea for more delicate foods (like white-fleshed fish) and more assertive teas—such as black and Lapsang souchong—with oily fish, chicken, and meats. Use loose-leaf tea, which burns more readily than powdered tea.

Other Ingredients

You can smoke with whole spices, such as peppercorns, allspice, and juniper berries, as well as with dried herbs, dried citrus peel, or even rice. These can be used on their own, but I've found that they're best used in concert with wood chips or tea, which will provide a good, evenly smoldering base that you bolster with the other aromatics.

SMOKED AND GRILLED HOT DOGS

I'm an absolute hot dog fanatic. It's probably due to my New Jersey upbringing—the state is home to some of the country's best roadside hot dog stands.

Most hot dog aficionados prefer the juicy snap of a dog in a natural casing. I do as well, but when smoking or grilling hot dogs—or, as in this case, both—I go for skinless, which allow the meat to absorb more of the smoky flavor. A quick stovetop smoke is an excellent way to add some complexity to any old dog, and finishing it on the grill crisps it up. I like to grill mine until they're very blistered and just beginning to burst.

As far as condiments and garnishes go, who am I to tell you how to eat your hot dog? You know how you like it.

MAKES 8 HOT DOGS

8 skinless hot dogs

8 hot dog buns, split

Assorted toppings and condiments

Soaked oak or fruit wood chips

1. Prepare a wood chip packet (see page 49) using soaked oak or fruit wood chips. Place the packet in the bottom of an indoor smoker, baking pan, or wok. Set a wire rack over the chips and put the pan over medium heat. When the chips begin to smoke, arrange the hot dogs on the rack and cover the pan with a tight-fitting lid or aluminum foil. Turn off the heat and smoke the hot dogs for 10 minutes, then remove from the smoke.

2. Meanwhile, prepare a medium-hot single-layer fire in a grill (see page 149) or heat a grill pan or skillet over medium-high heat.

3. Grill the hot dogs until charred to your liking (they're already cooked through, so this step is purely for flavor).

4. Serve the hot dogs in the buns with your choice of toppings and condiments.

SMOKED MACKEREL WITH HERB SPREAD AND GRILLED TOMATO CONCASSÉ

This is my ode to the quintessential New York breakfast: a spread of toasted bagels, cream cheese, and smoked fish. You can apply this smoking technique to any type of oily fish: salmon, trout, bluefish, and so on. I recommend smoking double the amount called for here and using the leftovers for a pâté or salad.

MAKES 4 SERVINGS

2 cups kosher salt

1 cup packed dark brown sugar

2 teaspoons freshly ground black pepper

3 bay leaves, crumbled

12 thyme sprigs, finely chopped

4 mackerel fillets (about 1 pound total)

2 hard-boiled eggs, thinly sliced

1 small red onion, halved and very thinly sliced

Herb Spread (recipe follows)

1 cup Grilled Tomato Concassé (recipe follows)

Toasted rye bread, for serving

Soaked oak or fruit wood chips

1 In a small bowl, combine the salt, sugar, pepper, bay leaves, and thyme and mix well. Put the mackerel fillets in a shallow dish and coat on both sides with the cure, packing it on well. Cover and refrigerate for 1 hour.

2 Remove the mackerel from the cure and rinse under cold water, then pat dry with paper towels.

3 Prepare a wood chip packet (see page 49) using soaked oak or fruit wood chips. Place the packet in the bottom of an indoor smoker, baking pan, or wok. Set a wire rack over the chips and put the pan over medium heat. When the chips begin to smoke, arrange the mackerel, skin side down, on the rack and cover the pan with a tight-fitting lid or aluminum foil. Smoke the mackerel over low heat until the flesh is firm and beginning to brown around the edges, 15 to 20 minutes. Turn off the heat and leave the mackerel in the smoker, covered, for 10 minutes.

4 Remove the mackerel from the smoker and separate the flesh into large chunks; discard the skin. Arrange the mackerel on a platter, along with the hard-boiled eggs, shaved onion, herb spread, tomato concassé, and a stack of rye toast.

continued

HERB SPREAD

Makes 1 cup

4 ounces cream cheese, at room temperature

½ cup crème fraîche

1 tablespoon chopped chives

1 tablespoon chopped parsley

1 tablespoon chopped tarragon

1 teaspoon chopped thyme

Kosher salt and freshly ground black pepper

In a bowl, stir together the cream cheese and crème fraîche until blended. Stir in the chives, parsley, tarragon, and thyme. Season to taste with salt and pepper. The herb spread can be refrigerated for up to 1 day.

GRILLED TOMATO CONCASSÉ

Makes about 1 cup

4 plum tomatoes, halved lengthwise

1 teaspoon extra–virgin olive oil, plus more for grilling the tomatoes

Kosher salt and freshly ground black pepper

1½ teaspoons sherry vinegar

½ teaspoon honey

1 garlic clove, finely chopped

½ teaspoon ground coriander

① Preheat a grill pan over high heat.

② Rub the tomatoes with olive oil and sprinkle with salt and pepper. Grill, cut side down, turning once, until well charred on both sides, about 2 minutes per side. Lower the heat and continue cooking the tomatoes, turning them once, until softened and collapsed, 15 to 20 minutes. Transfer to a cutting board and let cool slightly.

③ Peel the tomatoes and chop the flesh until almost pureed. Transfer to a bowl and stir in the 1 teaspoon olive oil, vinegar, honey, garlic, and coriander. Season to taste with salt and pepper. The concassé can be refrigerated for up to 1 day.

LESSON № 9 | BEER IS A CRAFT

I'M DRAWN TO BEER because it reminds me of cooking. Beer is essentially food: it starts with grain that is roasted, then cooked in water seasoned with anything you can dream up to throw in the pot. The only thing separating beer from a bowl of oatmeal is fermentation (compare beer and bread, and the similarities only increase). There's a reactive component in brewing beer that makes it more akin to cooking than to making wine or spirits. You begin making beer by following recipes, then grow comfortable enough to riff and experiment and, eventually, brew from instinct, experience, and touch. A great brewer is like a brilliant chef—he comes up with techniques and flavor combinations that absolutely blow your mind.

Beer is generally much easier to pair with food than wine (and a hell of a lot easier than whiskey). You don't have to think about tannins, and most beer is effervescent, which makes any beverage more food-friendly. Because beer and food have so much in common, you may find the same ingredients and flavors in the glass as on your plate.

I don't have any strict beer-pairing rules with barbecue or grilled foods; I think that people put way too much emphasis on that, as if you're going to unlock some secret flavors if you match your meal with the right beer. Your favorite beers will work alongside pretty much anything you cook over a live fire. The only time pairing gets tricky is when you're working with high levels of hops or alcohol. Generally speaking, I lean toward what are known as "session" beers with grilled or smoked meat. This loosely defined category includes anything crisp and light—5 percent alcohol by volume (ABV) or less—with a good balance of malt and hops. I.e., a beer you can drink all afternoon long. If I'm in the mood for a darker brew, I'll try a brown ale or a light-bodied English stout.

I also use beer a lot in cooking, and it's an important ingredient in many of my favorite condiments and side dishes. Cooking with beer is as easy as pairing it: just stay away from extra-hoppy or especially-high-alcohol brews, and don't reduce it too much, or it can get bitter.

FAVORITE BEER PRODUCERS

Since we opened Spuyten Duyvil, I've been able to see how a beer drinker's preferences evolve over time. Craft-beer newcomers typically gravitate toward big, bold-flavored beers at first—a reaction, most likely, to the weak sauce they've been drinking all their lives. (A similar thing happens when one begins drinking "good" wine.) Over time, however, the beer drinker starts seeking out more complexity and subtlety and begins hunting around the fringes of craft beer for new flavors and experiences. If enough people are evolving as drinkers at the same time, the zeitgeist shifts and you'll see the market respond to give them what they want. We're at a high point in craft beer right now, especially in America, where experimentation is contagious, old brewing recipes and practices are being resurrected, and more people are drinking better beer than they were the day before.

Below I've organized my favorite brewers by country. This list is in no way comprehensive, and if I were to revisit it a year from now, it would probably be noticeably different—that's how quickly the industry is growing and changing.

America

Thirty years ago, there was practically zero craft beer culture in America. Then in 1979, Jimmy Carter signed a bill that legalized home brewing, opening the way for a microbrewing revolution. Over the past two decades, the number of microbreweries in our country has climbed into the thousands. Our craft beer industry was born out of home brewing, which explains a few things about today's most popular style of beer—the hoppy pale ale. But one thing most brewers won't admit is that the hoppy West Coast IPA and extra-hoppy, high-alcohol Imperial IPA styles were reborn out of a couple of old home-brewing tricks. First, ales are a lot easier and faster to make than lager: ale yeast ferments at around room temperature, while lager yeast ferments at cooler temperatures and takes longer to do its work (the word *lager* is derived from the German word *lagern*, meaning "to store"). One is clearly a better fit for making in your kitchen or garage. Plus, when you make a beer that has flaws (which is very easy to do when brewing on a small scale), you can mask them by loading the beer with hops. The hops grown on the West Coast have especially intense bitterness and citrus flavors, so the first waves of American microbrews were dominated by hoppy, hedonistic ales. More recently, however, we've seen American brewers breaking out of the ale rut and trying new styles—some of them adapted from Europe, some resurrected from very old recipes, and some completely brand-new.

ALLAGASH BREWING COMPANY (PORTLAND, MAINE): This brewery has been in operation since 1995, which makes it an elder in the industry. Founder Rob Tod's Belgian-style beers have introduced many American drinkers to the category, but instead of settling into his success, he's continued to experiment and innovate with new fermentation, bottling, and aging techniques.

THE BRUERY (PLACENTIA, CALIFORNIA): This young brewery out of Orange County epitomizes craft beer at its best. They make a variety of styles, from saisons to giant barrel-aged beers and everything in between, including one of my favorite re-creations of *Berliner Weisse*, a sour wheat-based brew that dates back to the sixteenth century. Saison is the oldest style of beer still being made today.

CAPTAIN LAWRENCE BREWING COMPANY (ELMSFORD, NEW YORK): This was the first local microbrewery to be taken seriously by the beer world. In addition to a portfolio of popular ales, it turns out interesting new specialty beers each year.

CARTON BREWING (ATLANTIC HIGHLANDS, NEW JERSEY): This new brewery from my home state is blazing a trail by creating unique styles of beer, like Boat Beer, a low-alcohol session ale, and Monkey Chased the Weasel, flavored with mulberries.

CROOKED STAVE (DENVER, COLORADO): This brewery specializes in fermenting and aging beer in wood barrels, an old-school style of brewing that results in unique products.

EARTH, BREAD + BREWERY (PHILADELPHIA, PENNSYLVANIA): Tom Baker earned his reputation as one of America's great brewers at Heavyweight Brewing in New Jersey, which produced big, bold beers until he closed it down in 2006. He's resurfaced at this brewpub-bakery, where he bakes flatbread in a hand-built oven and serves a rotating selection of his beers.

HILL FARMSTEAD BREWERY (GREENSBORO, VERMONT): Shaun Hill is only in his mid-thirties, but he's already considered one of the world's top brewers because of the farmhouse ales he produces on his family's ancestral farm.

JOLLY PUMPKIN ARTISAN ALES (DEXTER, MICHIGAN): This was one of the first American breweries to get into barrel aging and play around with open fermentation. Almost the entire beer-making process is conducted in wood there, which results in a variety of complex, idiosyncratic brews.

KELSO BEER (BROOKLYN, NEW YORK): Brewer Kelly Taylor has been part of the microbrew scene since the early 1990s, but he didn't open his own operation until 2006. He chose to specialize in lagers, rather than the usual ales, which is still rare for a microbrewer.

PEEKSKILL BREWERY (PEEKSKILL, NEW YORK): This upstate brewery makes a range of great beer styles, most notably Hop Common, which is their version of "steamed beer," a lager made with yeast that ferments at higher temperatures.

PRAIRIE ARTISAN ALES (TULSA, OKLAHOMA): There are more and more great craft breweries popping up around the South, and Prairie is arguably the best. They make a wide range of both ales and stouts.

TIRED HANDS BREWING COMPANY (ARDMORE, PENNSYLVANIA): This new brewpub makes such a limited amount of beer that they only sell it at their bar, so you'll have to visit the Philadelphia suburbs if you want to try some. They riff a million ways on the saison style of beer, resulting in some very original brews.

Belgium

If it weren't for Belgium, America's craft beer revolution would have been drastically different, since so many American craft beers are interpretations of classic Belgian styles. Belgium itself has been relatively quiet on the craft beer front, though there are still a few small producers pushing the envelope. A handful of these producers make lambic, a very specific style made in Brussels and the Pajottenland region southwest of the city, which is one of my favorite beers. It's the beer version of natural wine, made using wild yeast and spontaneous fermentation and preserved with aged hops. The result is funky, acidic, and often sour. Bad lambic can taste like fruity soda, but the best producers make beer with an unmatched complexity.

BRASSERIE CANTILLON (ANDERLECHT): This lambic producer's brewery is literally a living museum—the facility has barely changed since it opened in 1900. It produces some of the world's best versions of *gueuze* (sparkling beer made by bottling a blend of three lambics and letting the beer undergo a secondary fermentation in the bottle) and *kriek* (lambic steeped with fruit), both made in an aggressive, feral style.

BRASSERIE DE LA SENNE (BRUSSELS): This newish venture by Yvan De Baets and Bernard Leboucq, both veteran brewers, makes a variety of excellent beers in a drier low-alcohol style.

BRASSERIE FANTÔME (SOY): This small farmhouse-based operation was the first Belgian producer to get creative with saison, the style of farmhouse ale that originated in the French-speaking Wallonia region in southern Belgium.

BROUWERIJ DE RANKE (WEVELGEM): This was the first Belgian brewery to use a high amount of hops, including American-grown varieties, in its ales.

BROUWERIJ DRIE FONTEINEN (BEERSEL): If there's a Petrus of lambic, it's Drie Founteinen. This brewery blends its own lambic with lambic it sources from other brewers to make unmatched *gueuzes* and *krieks*.

Germany

Historically, every town in Germany had its own brewery, and the locals drank its beer and its beer only. It was not until refrigeration was invented that breweries began shipping their wares around the country. Lagers became the predominant style, and Munich became the country's beer hub. Today there are only a few independent breweries left—most others are owned by large conglomerates—but some of these producers are breaking out of Germany's stubborn stylistically strict brewing mold.

FREIGEIST AND THE MONARCHY (COLOGNE): Sebastian Sauer is one of the few new craft brewers in Germany who isn't specializing in traditional styles. Among his bottlings are imperial stouts, *Gose* (*gueuze*), a peat-smoked porter, and several ancient recipes that he's resurrected under his Monarchy label.

KLOSTER ANDECHS (ANDECHS): This gorgeous monastery west of Munich brews a range of traditional German beers. All are awesome, but their shining achievement is *Doppelbock*, a big, full-bodied lager with the purest malt flavor of any I've ever tasted.

MAHRS-BRÄU (BAMBERG): The Bavarian town of Bamberg is a hub of German brewing, most famously known as the home of *Rauchbier* (smoked beer), which is made with malted barley that's been dried over a fire. But Mahrs-Bräu doesn't make this style; its specialty is *Ungespundet*, their version of *Kellerbier*, a hazy, unfiltered style of ale that has been matured in air-exposed casks, which darken the color and add complexity.

PROFESSOR FRITZ BRIEM (FRIESING): Fritz Briem was a professor at Weihenstephan, the oldest brewing school in world. He started his eponymous label to re-create long-forgotten styles of German beers, including a *Berliner Weisse* and *Grut Bier*, a thirteenth-century style with rosemary, anise, bay leaves, and other spices.

Elsewhere

BRASSERIE DES FRANCHES-MONTAGNES (SAIGNELÉGIER, SWITZERLAND): In 1997, winemaker Jérôme Rebetez turned his attention to beer by opening this brewery, where he specializes in bold, assertively flavored beers made using nontraditional techniques and ingredients. He was the first producer I know of to make a high-alcohol barrel-aged beer that's bone-dry: the Abbaye de Saint Bon-Chien, a sour, wine-like brew.

DIEU DU CIEL! (QUEBEC, CANADA): This brewpub in Montreal's Mile End borrows styles from around Europe and America to make a prolific range of bold, innovative beers.

HOPFENSTARK (QUEBEC, CANADA): Located about thirty miles north of Montreal, this microbrewery is another example of microbrew new wave. They make a little bit of everything from low-alcohol *Berliner Weisse* to boozy Imperial stouts.

WILD BEER CO. (WESTCOMBE, ENGLAND): There are lots of traditional English breweries that produce beers I love, but very few that go against the grain. Most notable among England's microbreweries is the Wild Beer Co. Many of its beers are based on the Belgian saison style, made using spontaneous fermentation and a host of unconventional ingredients like cucumber and American hops.

Gypsy Brewers

For a long time, contract brewing—that is, hiring other facilities to make your beer—was seen as a bad thing, with the assumption that you couldn't control the quality of your product. But these itinerate "gypsy" brewers have turned that notion on its head by making one-off, small-batch, highly experimental beers all over the world.

EVIL TWIN BREWING: Jeppe Jarnit-Bjergsø (pictured below) started his gypsy brewing operation in his native Denmark, then relocated to Brooklyn, where he has dreamt up a panoply of cleverly named beers like Katz Pis and Ashtray Heart, including custom house beers for top restaurants like Copenhagen's Noma and his own Brooklyn restaurant, Tørst.

LOCAL OPTION: This Chicago brewery partners with other breweries to make a range of historic and almost forgotten styles of beer, like the Kentucky Common, a tart, dark pre-Prohibition–style ale made at Louisville's Against the Grain brewery.

MIKKELLER: Mikkel Borg Bjergsø got into gypsy brewing a few years ahead of his twin brother, Jeppe (see Evil Twin Brewing, above). He has made hundreds of beers in dozens of countries, and each project breaks new ground or challenges our notion of what beer is.

STILLWATER ARTISANAL ALES: Based in Baltimore, this gypsy brewer is stylistically more focused than others in the category. It concentrates on making saison beers, which it augments in countless interesting ways.

LESSON № 10

FIRE EQUALS FLAVOR

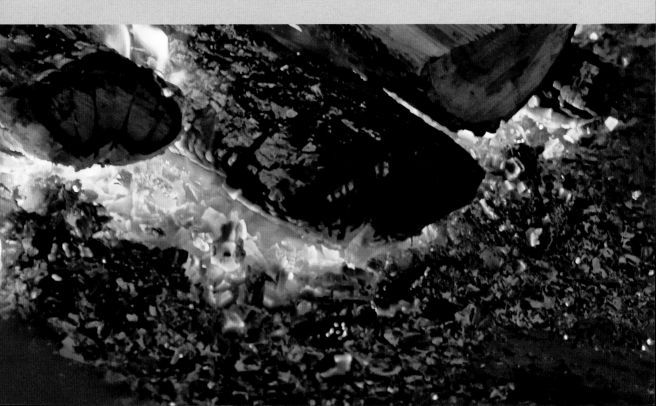

THE SECRET TO great grilling lies in the char, something only a hot grill can deliver. It can transform an ordinary piece of meat or fish into something deeply primal tasting, with a textural harmony that drives carnivores crazy: a crunchy, burnished crust and a juicy, tender interior.

Unfortunately, most cooks are afraid to give food the char it deserves. They equate char with burnt food, but the two are distinctly different: Burnt food is completely carbonized and tastes acrid and unpleasant. Char is deep caramelization on a food's surface, that smoky-sweet flavor we associate with live-fire cooking; without it, you might as well stand at the stove.

People also get too hung up on creating perfect crosshatched grill marks on their meat. While this looks great in photographs, they're missing out on a lot of surface area that could be charred; this is why I prefer to move and turn meat frequently while making sure that as much of its surface touches the hot grill grates as possible. A steak charred all over tastes significantly better than one with a few black stripes. And this flavor gets even better when you add charcoal to the equation, but I'm getting ahead of myself. First you need to pick a grill.

CHOOSE YOUR GRILL

Gas or charcoal? Choosing a grill begins with the all-important question of fuel. While you can make the recipes in this book using a gas grill, grill pan, or, hell, even a George Foreman "grill," grilling without charcoal is like playing bluegrass without a banjo: something will be unmistakably absent. I've already emphasized the importance of using hardwood charcoal when barbecuing—there's no substitute for the flavor it adds to smoked meat. The same goes for grilling. While it's true that nothing can compete with the convenience of a gas grill, it's also true that nothing can compete with the flavor of charcoal-grilled food.

Gas Grills

Gas grills can be lit with the push of a button and are ready to start cooking in a few minutes, and you never have to worry about tending a fire or adding more fuel (until the propane tank runs out). The cooking temperature is both more consistent and easier to adjust with gas, you can easily create two or more heat zones, and there is far less cleanup when you're finished. Many gas grills also have neat accessories and add-ons, like side burners, warming racks, and rotisseries. For all of these reasons, most home cooks opt for gas grills.

However, gas grills lose out to charcoal in two important categories: First, most gas grills can't get nearly as hot as even the cheapest charcoal grill, which means food won't get enough char before it's cooked through. A commercial gas grill can get as hot as charcoal, yes, but most of the four-wheeled contraptions sitting on our decks and patios don't come close. More important, you're missing out on a key ingredient when you cook with gas: charcoal. Carbonized wood is more than just fuel: it imparts its own flavor, a smokiness we associate with backyard cookouts, feasts on the beach, summertime gatherings, and a host of other food memories. The smoke produced by burning charcoal is different from that produced by burning gas: Gas smoke is basically flavorless, charcoal smoke contains more compounds that contribute flavor.

If a gas grill makes more sense for you, though, buy one! What you might lose in flavor you'll make up for in speed and ease.

Charcoal Grills

Grilling over charcoal has a visceral appeal—think of steaks sizzling over a pile of glowing, smoldering coals—that a gas grill can't match. And charcoal grills are far cheaper than gas ones. Your main consideration when choosing a charcoal grill should be size: it should be able to accommodate two or more heat zones, a setup that's needed (or at least helpful) for cooking many of the recipes in this book. For kettle grills, look for a diameter of 20 inches or larger; most barrel- or box-shaped charcoal grills are wide enough for multistage grilling. If you plan to barbecue on your grill, bigger is better, so the meat won't be too close to the heat source.

You can actually eliminate the need for multizone cooking by using a charcoal grill that lets you raise and lower the grate over the coals to fine-tune the cooking temperature. Argentinean-style grills (see Resources, page 255), which are in this category, are operated by crank. A simpler style of adjustable grill is the Tuscan grill (see Resources), which has a grate that can rest on two or three different levels of rungs. The best thing about a Tuscan grill is its portability—I take mine anywhere there might be a live fire and some food to cook: weekend getaways, campgrounds, beaches; it even works in a fireplace.

Your next consideration should be the grilling grate itself. I prefer a standard wire grate to wide metal or cast-iron bars: more space between the bars allows more airflow and more direct heat to reach your food, which helps brown the entire surface, not just what's touching the grate. You should also look for grates that have hinged sections that allow you to add or move charcoal and wood without having to remove the entire grate.

Two more essentials: The grill should have two vents—one in the base and one in the lid—for controlling airflow and, thus, heat. And it should have enough headspace to accommodate large pieces of meat or whole poultry when the grill is covered.

Beyond that, choose a model that suits your individual needs and budget. My workhorse is the Weber One-Touch, a simple kettle grill that cost about $100 and has never failed me.

ORGANIZE YOUR EQUIPMENT

There's an entire industry built around grilling gadgets (what else are we supposed to get our dads for Father's Day?). But you need only a few simple tools to get you on the path to grilling greatness.

Chimney Starter

A charcoal fire begins with a chimney starter (see page 148). Better yet, buy two of them: one to fill your grill with an initial load of coals and another to keep extra coals ready for replenishing, or to dump two loads of charcoal into the grill for an extra-hot fire.

Instant-Read Thermometer

If you want to cook meat properly, you need a reliable thermometer—there's just no way around it. Buy the fastest and most accurate thermometer you can afford. My favorite, the ThermoWorks Thermapen, runs around $100 but pays for itself quickly when you consider how many expensive pieces of meat it will prevent you from overcooking. It reads internal temperature within 3 seconds and 1°F of accuracy, which is about a thousand times better than a standard dial thermometer (which I don't trust). There are cheaper instant-read thermometers on the market, but whatever you buy, check its speed and accuracy by testing it in a pot of boiling water: it should register 212°F within a few seconds. If it doesn't, get a better thermometer.

Wire Brush

A stiff wire brush will help you clean your grates before and after grilling. Look for one with a long, sturdy handle and a built-in scraper for tackling any stuck food particles. Brush the grates once they have heated up, then grab a rolled-up towel or wad of paper towels with a pair of tongs, dip it in water, and wipe the grates clean before oiling the grate and cooking. Repeat this process after you've finished grilling to keep the grates gunk- and rust-free.

Tongs

Most tongs designed for grilling are worthlessly flimsy. Long-handled, V-shaped, spring-loaded kitchen tongs are much better. Keep at least two pairs handy whenever you grill: one for handling charcoal and lifting the grate and another for moving food around on the grill.

Heavy-Duty Gloves

I keep a pair of heavy rubber gloves handy whenever I'm smoking or grilling larger pieces of meat that can't be easily moved with tongs. Fireproof leather gloves are also handy for handling hot chimney starters and for shielding your hands from heat when brushing food or moving it around the grill.

Basting Brush

I don't do a ton of basting when I grill meat, but for recipes that do require basting or brushing, a long-handled brush with silicone bristles is best: the bristles won't catch fire and they can be cleaned more easily than natural bristles.

Spray Bottle

A few flames licking at your food is fine, but especially fatty meats will create the occasional flare-up, which can scorch your food and make it taste burnt. A cheap spray bottle will extinguish any flare-ups; use one with an adjustable nozzle set to the thinnest stream possible.

Ash Can

Ashes are a grill's worst enemy. They absorb heat, get blown onto food, and, if they get wet, turn into cement that is hard to remove. Always remove any leftover coals and ashes after you've finished grilling and dump them into a metal ash can with a lid. Once they are completely cool, the ashes can be dumped into the trash.

Grill Cover

An uncovered grill will quickly become a rusty, ruined one. Buy a cover that will shield it from the elements.

MARYLAND PIT BEEF

American barbecue is a working-class food. Although these days we eat much of our smoked meat in the comfort of restaurants that offer craft beer and accept American Express, our nation's greatest culinary contribution was born out of keeping hardworking folks fed.

Baltimore's offering to the barbecue canon—pit beef—is no exception. Originating in roadside shacks in Charm City's blue-collar neighborhoods, the pit beef sandwich—like its cousins in Chicago (Italian beef sandwich), Los Angeles (French dip), and Buffalo (beef on weck)—comprises a roll heaped high with thinly sliced beef. But that's where the similarities end. Baltimore pit beef gets its distinctive smoky flavor from a charcoal fire, which results in a deeply charred exterior and a juicy interior. The preferred serving vessel in Baltimore is a kaiser roll—a nod to the city's Eastern European roots—and its signature garnishes are slices of raw white onion and a punchy blend of mayonnaise and horseradish known as "tiger sauce."

When the city's industrial economy was still strong, there was a stretch of pit beef joints along the Pulaski Highway, but only a few remain today. The best-known survivor of this pit beef corridor is Chaps (see Resources, page 255), a white shack that shares a parking lot with a strip club. There, owner Bob Creager, a former steelworker, burns through 200 pounds of charcoal a day while cooking a butcher's-case selection of meats and sausages on his indoor pit. But most folks come here for the pit beef, which Creager makes by first searing large hunks of bottom round over a hot fire, then letting it cook to temperature (your choice, though most folks ask for medium rare) over low heat. The beef is shaved to order on a meat slicer and piled onto a kaiser roll to make a true two-handed sandwich.

You'll also find great pit beef just west of the city in Woodlawn at Pioneer Pit Beef, an address-less yellow hut tucked below Interstate 70 (see Resources, page 255). The menu at Pioneer is far shorter than Chaps' (beef, ham, pork, or turkey), as are its hours of operation (11 A.M. to 5 P.M.), and the beef—also made from bottom round here—has a more intense smokiness. Beyond that, the folks at Pioneer won't tell you much about their craft. But in true deli fashion, the counterperson will hand you the first piece of freshly sliced meat for approval before making your sandwich.

Is pit beef barbecue? While it is cooked over direct heat, it cooks for a considerable amount of time over low heat and its predominant flavor comes from smoke. I say it's more barbecue than grilled meat. But if you ask anyone in Baltimore, they'll say it's neither: it's just pit beef.

MARYLAND-STYLE PIT BEEF

Most pit-beef joints use top round, which is painfully lean and pretty bland. Top sirloin, which is much fattier, makes for a better-tasting sandwich and is worth the extra few bucks. You'll want to trim any large pieces of fat from the outside of the roast before you cook it— render it and save the delicious fat for cooking potatoes. It's important to stop cooking the beef just as it hits the rare zone; the searing and carryover cooking will bring it up to somewhere between rare and medium-rare, which is the ideal doneness for slicing. The longer grilling process means wood—be it chips, chunks, or logs—will have time to contribute flavor, and it should be used in addition to charcoal or gas.

MAKES ENOUGH FOR 16 TO 20 SANDWICHES

One 10-pound top sirloin roast	½ teaspoon cayenne pepper
¼ cup kosher salt	16 to 20 kaiser rolls, split
1 tablespoon freshly ground black pepper	Tiger Sauce (recipe follows)
1 tablespoon paprika	2 white onions, thinly sliced
1 teaspoon garlic powder	
1 teaspoon dried oregano	Wood chunks or soaked wood chips
1 teaspoon ground cumin	

① Use a sharp paring knife to trim any papery silver skin from the sirloin. Trim off any large chunks of hard fat (see the headnote). You might also find a couple of small strips of meat or two hanging off the roast by some connective tissue; trim these off as well, as they'll end up tough and chewy if cooked. Use a large knife to cut the sirloin lengthwise in half.

② In a small bowl, combine the salt, pepper, paprika, garlic powder, oregano, cumin, and cayenne pepper. Rub the spice blend all over the meat, making sure to get into the cracks and crevices. Wrap the 2 sirloin halves in plastic and refrigerate for at least 1 hour, and up to overnight.

③ Prepare a two-stage fire with hot and cool sides in a grill (see page 149). Unwrap the meat and prepare a wood chip packet (see page 49).

④ Place the wood chip packet or wood chunks over the coals and place the roast on the cool side of the grill. Cover the grill and cook the meat, turning it over after 30 minutes, until an instant-read thermometer inserted into the middle of the roast registers 115°F, about 1 hour.

⑤ Transfer the roast to the hot side of the grill and sear until well charred on all sides, about 5 minutes per side. Transfer to a cutting board and let rest for 10 to 15 minutes.

⑥ Slice the meat as thin as possible (if you have a meat slicer, use it!) and pile onto the kaiser rolls. Serve with the sauce and sliced onions.

> **NOTE**
>
> The beef can be cooked up to 1 day ahead, cooled, then wrapped in plastic and refrigerated. Slice and serve cold or wrap in foil and rewarm in a 200°F oven.

continued

TIGER SAUCE

MAKES ABOUT 2 CUPS

2 garlic cloves

1 teaspoon kosher salt

1 cup prepared
horseradish

1 cup mayonnaise

2 teaspoons fresh
lemon juice

1 teaspoon freshly
ground black pepper

Using the side of a heavy knife, mash the garlic
cloves with a pinch of salt into a paste on a
cutting board. Transfer to a small bowl, add
the horseradish, mayonnaise, lemon juice, the
remaining salt, and the pepper, and whisk to
combine. The sauce can be refrigerated for up
to 4 days.

LESSON NO. 11 | CHARCOAL: KEEP IT PURE

AT HOME, I MOSTLY use hardwood charcoal for grilling, often in concert with hardwood chunks or wood chips to add more wood-smoke flavor. As far as store-bought charcoal is concerned, there's hardwood lump charcoal and there's everything else. Pure hardwood charcoal is black, chalky, and irregularly shaped. It's made by slowly burning wood in a controlled low-oxygen environment until it's almost completely carbonized. When lit, these lumps burn cleanly and evenly and impart a bit of smoky flavor to food. Some say hardwood charcoal burns hotter than briquettes, but *Cook's Illustrated* magazine and others have found this to be true only when measuring charcoal by weight, not by volume (that is, a chimney-full of briquettes will be just as hot as a chimney-full of hardwood charcoal). However, hardwood charcoal does burn faster than briquettes, as it's less compact, so you'll need to replenish the coals more often if grilling for longer periods of time. Although you can sometimes find hardwood charcoal made from a specific wood, most is made from scrap wood of unknown provenance. I haven't found "varietal" charcoal to contribute any noticeable flavor difference, though charcoal that is all made from the same type of wood probably burns more evenly and consistently than charcoal made from assorted scraps.

Most backyard cooks still use charcoal briquettes, which were invented in the late nineteenth century and commercialized by Henry Ford, who teamed up with E. G. Kingsford to turn Ford's car-manufacturing wooden scraps into charcoal. Briquettes are made by burning sawdust and wood chips, then mixing the carbonized wood with binders and additives and molding them into uniformly shaped pillows. The "other" stuff in charcoal briquettes varies from one brand to the next, but it often includes sodium nitrate, mineral coal, starch, and fresh sawdust. The main advantage briquettes have over lump charcoal is the consistency at which they burn, which is more slowly and more evenly than hardwood. Briquettes also produce a lot more ash, which can insulate the coals and lower their heat output. I prefer hardwood charcoal to briquettes for the same reason I like mortadella more than bologna: the flavor is more pure and natural and there's a lot less mystery. Whichever you choose, stay far away from any briquettes impregnated with lighter fluid or other accelerants; these will definitely add nasty flavors to your food.

Before we bought our fuel charcoal in paper bags, we Americans simply burned logs down into coals, then grilled over them. That is still the best fuel for grilling by

far, though it's also the least practical and most time-consuming: not only do you know exactly where your fuel comes from, you will also get more wood-smoke flavor. Making your own coals is as easy as building a fire in your grill and waiting until the logs become coals.

BUILDING A CHARCOAL FIRE

If you have a chimney starter, begin by loosely crumpling up a couple sheets of newspaper and drizzling or spraying them with vegetable oil (this will make them burn longer and will speed up the charcoal lighting process). Stuff the newspaper into the lower chamber. Remove the grill's top grate (where the food will be placed) and set it aside; put the chimney starter on the grill's bottom grate. Fill it with charcoal, light the newspaper, and let the charcoal burn until the coals are glowing red and coated in gray ash, about 15 minutes. (You can speed the process by blowing on the chimney with a hair dryer; the extra air flow will make the coals ignite more quickly.) Carefully dump the charcoal onto the bottom grate into your desired arrangement (see opposite), then replace the top grate.

If you don't have a chimney starter, remove the grill's bottom grate and place some crumpled newspaper in the bottom of the grill. Drizzle the paper with vegetable oil, cover it with the grate, and add a pile of charcoal. Light the newspaper and let the charcoal burn until it's covered in gray ash, then scatter it into your desired arrangement.

Once you have a layer of glowing coals in your grill, you can add another layer of unlit charcoal on top. You'll want to do this when using a large or deep kettle grill or when you want to create a deeper bed of coals for hotter direct-heat grilling. Then wait until the new charcoal has ignited before grilling. If you're using hardwood charcoal, you can throw a few lumps onto burning coals anytime during the grilling process. With briquettes, be sure to let them ignite and burn until they're ashen (to burn off the bad-tasting chemicals) before cooking over them.

I've also used a chimney starter as a makeshift grill by placing a grate directly on top of the burning coals. This is good for quickly searing a tuna steak or any other protein that you only want to char on the outside without cooking the interior.

Arranging the Charcoal

There are numerous ways to set up a charcoal fire, depending on what you're cooking and how much heat you need. I usually create two zones for grilling: a hot or medium-hot side for searing and charring food and a low-heat or completely cool (charcoal-free) side for cooking thicker cuts of meat and indirect grilling.

SINGLE-LEVEL FIRE

Spread an even layer of charcoal, about one or two coals deep, over the bottom of the grill. This will create a medium- to medium-hot fire, depending on the thickness of the coals, that is best for direct cooking of ingredients that would burn over a hotter fire, such as vegetables and fish. If you are cooking thinner cuts of meat or other foods that need only a quick spell on the grill, you can make a deeper bed of coals to create a scorching-hot fire.

TWO-STAGE FIRE

You can create two heat zones by adding different amounts of coals to each side of the grill (or leaving one half of the grill coal-free to create a cool side). For a hot zone, build a layer about two coals deep; for medium, one coal deep; for low, scatter a few coals evenly over that side; and for cool, use no coals at all.

MULTI-ZONE FIRE

If you have a large rectangular grill or large kettle grill, you can create hot, medium, and low zones by making two separate layers of coals (about two coals deep for high heat and a single layer of coals for medium) and leaving a third section devoid of charcoal. Use this setup when grilling a variety of foods at the same time.

HOW HOT IS THE GRILL?

There's no foolproof way to measure the heat of a charcoal fire. Even the most precise thermometers can only check the temperature of a specific spot, and even a perfectly uniform bed of coals will result in a range of constantly fluctuating temperatures as they burn, creating hotter and cooler spots above. (In this respect, gas grills have the advantage over charcoal in that you can adjust the heat with a knob, though gas grills also have hot spots.)

However, if you've ever followed a grilling recipe, you've probably come across the "hand test," in which you place your paw a few inches over the fire and count until the heat becomes unbearably painful. Fun, right? There are many reasons why the hand test is an inaccurate gauge of temperature at best and self-inflicted torture at worst. As I noted above, even a uniform fire will be hotter in spots and cooler in others. Also, everyone has a different pain threshold; one man's "medium" heat is another's "Shit, that's hot!"

For these reasons, I pay less attention to how hot a fire feels to my hand than how it affects the food I'm cooking over it. Instead, I use my other senses: I can *hear* the difference between high and low heat when I place food on the grill; I can *see* how quickly the food forms a charred crust, and I can *smell* it caramelize on the grill—and then begin to burn if the heat is too high.

That said, the hand test is, unfortunately, your best bet until you get accustomed to how much heat a given charcoal arrangement will produce. Just before you're ready to put the food on the grill, place your hand about 5 inches above the grate and count—or, better yet, look at your watch (we tend to count more quickly when our flesh is hovering over a scorching-hot fire). See how long you can comfortably hold your hand over the heat to determine how hot the fire is.

8-plus seconds = low heat

6 to 8 seconds = medium-low

4 to 6 seconds = medium

2 to 4 seconds = medium-hot

Less than 2 seconds = hot

LESSON NO 12 | OIL EARLY AND OIL WELL

BEFORE YOU PUT food on a hot grill, scrape off any leftover gunk with a wire brush. Then take a kitchen towel, roll it up into a tight cylinder, and tie it with twine. Grab a pair of tongs, dunk the towel into a bowl of vegetable oil, and rub down the grates. This first wipe-down cleans the grill. Wait a minute, then dunk the towel and wipe the grill again, and again a minute later, repeating the process until you've oiled the grill, about ten times if you're grilling a food that tends to stick, like fish or chicken. This repeated oiling may sound like OCD, but doing so really helps to create a nonstick seasoning on the grate that, like a cast-iron skillet, gets better and better over time. You don't have to be quite as fastidious if you're cooking something that won't stick— three or four rounds of wiping is sufficient for most other grilling tasks.

I also oil the food before it hits the grill. I lightly coat all vegetables and most fish evenly with olive oil, which, in addition to helping the ingredients cook evenly, infuses the food with flavor as it cooks. However, I don't think you should oil red meat before grilling: That makes it harder to achieve that great charred crust we glorified in Lesson 10. All but the leanest cuts of meat will start oozing fat the moment they hit the grill. If a steak, pork chop, or piece of chicken sticks to the grates when you try to turn it, you're flipping it too soon. Wait a minute, then try again; it'll release when it's ready.

When I'm finished using the grill, I rarely bother cleaning it beyond quickly scraping off any big chunks of stuff stuck to the grates. The last thing you want to do when a gorgeous meal is waiting for you is to stop to clean the grill meticulously. Leave the cleanup for after the meal, and go eat.

LESSON №13 | BRINING AND SALTING ARE
WORTH THE TIME

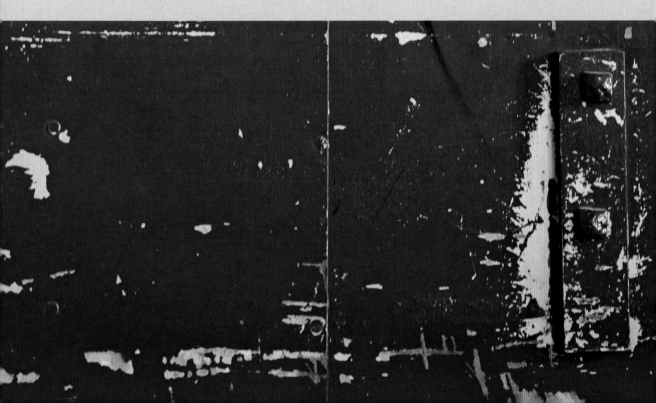

A WELL-MARBLED STEAK or lamb chop contains enough intramuscular fat to keep it juicy when cooked, but animals that carry more of their fat on the outside of their bodies—like chicken and pig—need your help to stay tender, flavorful, and juicy throughout, especially when their fate is a hot grill or smoker. You can do this in either of two ways: brining or salting ahead of time.

BRINING

You're probably already familiar with brines, but I've found that it often takes a little push to convince home cooks to actually take the plunge. Simply put, a brine penetrates muscle tissue over time through osmosis, and salt helps denature proteins in the meat, which ultimately trap the moisture within, preventing the meat from drying out as it cooks.

Your most basic brine is nothing more than saltwater (1 pound kosher salt to 1 gallon water), but I find this makes the meat just taste like the ocean, so I often employ other flavorful liquids, like bourbon, beer, or sweet tea, along with various sweeteners, herbs, spices, and other flavorings. I've also used Fette Sau's house dry rub as the base for a chicken brine (see page 160); all you need to do is add water. Whatever flavors you add to your brine, don't skimp. Remember that you're diluting these flavors with lots of water. Most brines can be mixed cold (just make sure you stir the brine until all of the salt and sugar have dissolved), but if a recipe calls for the brine to be boiled, let it cool to room temperature before using it.

The hardest part about brining is knowing how long to soak the meat. You want to wait long enough for the brine to do its work, but not so long that it continues breaking down protein to the point of mushiness. A spongy, overbrined pork chop is much worse than a nonbrined one. How long you brine depends on the type and size of the meat: pork and chicken parts should be brined for anywhere from 30 minutes (for thin cuts) to 6 hours (for thick cuts, chops, and tenderloins). Whole chickens need 4 to 8 hours, depending on their size; turkeys require about 1 hour per pound. And big pork roasts need about 2 hours per inch of thickness.

BRINING TIMES	WHOLE CHICKEN	4 to 8 hours (about 1 hour per pound)
	CHICKEN PIECES	30 minutes to 2 hours
	WHOLE TURKEY	12 to 24 hours (about 1 hour per pound)
	PORK CHOPS	2 to 6 hours or 8 to 12 hours for double-cut chops
	PORK TENDERLOIN	4 to 8 hours
	WHOLE PORK LOIN	24 hours

Many recipes call for overnight brining, which is excessive, and destructive, to all but the largest cuts of meat. It's better to err on the side of underbrining; you'll find that even a quick brine is better than none at all.

If you're brining chicken or other poultry and want its skin to crisp up while it cooks (you do!), then let the brined bird dry for a few hours before you cook it. The best way to do this is to place it atop a wire rack set over a baking sheet (or something else to catch any drippings) and refrigerate it until about an hour before you're ready to cook. Then let the bird come to room temperature while you prepare the grill or smoker.

I occasionally brine seafood before throwing it on the grill. I've found that 10 to 15 minutes in a simple brine will plump up a piece of fish and help it stay firm and moist when grilled. With oily fish like salmon, brining also helps prevent that foamy white albumin from creeping up through the flesh as the fish cooks. With shrimp and other shellfish, a quick brine is all you need to boost the flavor.

One very important thing to remember with any meat that's been brined: be careful about seasoning it during and after cooking. Cook the meat and taste it before adding any salt.

BASIC BRINE

This simple brine can be used with poultry or pork, and it can become the foundation for many new iterations. You can add a handful or two of aromatics (such as garlic, onions, herbs, spices, or citrus zest), replace some or all of the water with other liquids (such as beer or cider), or play around with sweeteners (try maple syrup, molasses, or honey).

MAKES 1 GALLON

1 cup kosher salt

½ cup granulated sugar or packed dark brown sugar

1 gallon water

In a stockpot, bring the salt, sugar, and 8 cups of the water to a boil, stirring until the salt and sugar have dissolved. Turn off the heat, add the remaining 8 cups water, and let the brine cool to room temperature before using.

SALTING

There are times when brines aren't practical or necessary (when cooking beef or lamb, for instance), but you still want your meat to be well seasoned before it hits the grill. That's when you should preseason with salt.

If I'm grilling steaks or lamb chops, I'll give them a generous shower of kosher salt as soon as I pull them out of the refrigerator. By the time I'm ready to grill, the salt will have begun to season and lightly tenderize the meat. The salt first draws out moisture from the meat (osmosis again), then seasons those juices, and eventually works its way back into the meat. This is not an instantaneous process, however: if you don't have at least 45 minutes for the salt to do its work, instead season the meat just before you put it on the grill. If you have a day or two and really want to season the meat throughout, you can dry-cure the meat by salting it (using about 1 teaspoon kosher salt per pound of meat) and placing it on a wire rack set over a baking sheet in the refrigerator, loosely covered with plastic wrap. Dry-curing works especially well with extra-thick steaks, roasts, and whole chickens.

Some Favorite Salts

I use coarse salt when I cook—never anything finer than kosher. Coarse salt is both easier to pick up and sprinkle over food and easier to see on whatever you're seasoning. It's much too easy to overseason with fine salt, which disappears as soon as it hits the meat.

Whatever I'm grilling, I like seasoning to be capricious; that is, I like flavors to appear in short, deliberate doses—a little hit of spiciness here, a bright acidic note there—rather than a homogeneous blend. Finishing salts give you little bursts of flavor that you can't get with just properly seasoned food. I like flaky Maldon salt, which is crunchy but delicate and dissolves rather quickly in your mouth, or a sea salt with the size and texture of raw sugar, such as fleur de sel, which also has a pleasant mineral flavor. Likewise, a few coarse grinds of black pepper punctuate the food with musky heat, plus pepper helps just about anything become more booze-friendly, be it beer, wine, or spirit.

BOURBON-BRINED CENTER-CUT PORK CHOPS

I'd given up on pork chops—always so dry and boring!—until I learned two ways to fix the problem: use a thick chop and brine it. This brine started as a sauce; I wanted to match bourbon's sweet malt and vanilla flavors with pork, so I added a splash to melted butter. It later morphed into a boozy brine that could also be used with chicken, and I combined both in this recipe. Cabin Still is a great cooking bourbon, but you can use the cheapest bottle you'd be willing to drink.

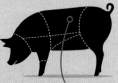

CENTER-CUT PORK CHOPS

MAKES 4 SERVINGS

BOURBON BRINE

1 gallon water

1 cup kosher salt

1 cup packed dark brown sugar

1 large yellow onion, thinly sliced

1 head garlic, halved horizontally

2 bay leaves

1 cinnamon stick, preferably Mexican

1 tablespoon black peppercorns

1 tablespoon allspice berries

1 tablespoon whole cloves

¾ cup olive oil

1½ cups bourbon

PORK CHOPS

4 bone-in center-cut pork chops (10 to 12 ounces each), about 1½ inches thick

4 tablespoons unsalted butter

1 tablespoon bourbon

Coarse sea salt

1 In a large pot, combine all of the brine ingredients except the bourbon and bring to a boil. Turn off the heat and stir in the bourbon. Let cool to room temperature, then transfer to a nonreactive container and refrigerate until cold.

2 Put the pork chops in the cold brine and refrigerate for 8 to 12 hours.

3 Remove the pork chops from the brine and pat dry with paper towels. Discard the brine.

4 Prepare a two-stage fire with medium and hot sides in a grill (see page 149), making sure to oil the grill grates well.

5 Grill the pork chops over high heat until well charred on both sides, 2 to 3 minutes per side. Then move the pork chops to the medium-heat side and grill, turning every few minutes, until an instant-read thermometer inserted horizontally into the center of the chops reads 145°F, 12 to 15 minutes longer. Transfer the pork to a platter and let rest for 5 minutes.

6 While the pork chops rest, in a small skillet, melt the butter over medium heat. Carefully add the bourbon and then tilt the pan away from you until it ignites (use a match or a lighter if using an electric stove). Let the alcohol burn off, then swirl the sauce until emulsified.

7 Transfer the pork chops to plates and spoon some of the sauce over each chop. Sprinkle with coarse salt and serve.

BARBECUED TURKEY

When done right, barbecued turkey is absolutely perfect—and it makes an unexpected addition to the Thanksgiving table. But turkey is a tricky bird to smoke, as the window between cooked through and overcooked is awfully small. Brining widens your margin of error by keeping the bird extra-moist, but make sure to treat your turkey like a sick patient and monitor its temperature carefully. The dry rub here is purely optional; use it if you want to give Thanksgiving dinner even more barbecue flavor.

WHOLE TURKEY

MAKES 10 TO 12 SERVINGS

1 whole turkey (12 to 14 pounds), preferably heritage breed

1 gallon Basic Brine (page 156)

1 cup Fette Sau Dry Rub (page 35; optional)

Wood chunks or soaked wood chips

1 Put the turkey in a large nonreactive container and cover with the brine; or use a brining bag. Refrigerate for 8 to 16 hours, turning the turkey over halfway through brining.

2 Set a wire rack on a rimmed baking sheet. Remove the turkey from the brine and rinse well; discard the brine. Pat the turkey dry with paper towels and put it on the wire rack. Refrigerate for 24 hours.

3 Remove the rack, leaving the turkey on the baking sheet, and coat it lightly all over with the dry rub, if using (you may not need all of the rub).

4 Preheat a smoker to 225°F or set up a grill for smoking (see page 44 or 47).

5 Place the turkey in the smoker and smoke, maintaining a smoker temperature between 200°F and 250°F, replenishing the wood chunks or chips as needed, until an instant-read thermometer inserted into the center of a leg registers 165°F. Total smoking time will be 6 to 7 hours. Transfer the turkey to a cutting board and let rest for 10 minutes before carving and serving.

DRY RUB-BRINED CHICKEN

Barbecue chicken is so common that we often overlook it. But when done well, it's one of my very favorites, and it's also one of the most forgiving meats to smoke. This recipe is based on the chicken I made at my first (and last) attempt at competition barbecue at Memphis in May (see page 167). I simply took our house dry rub and turned it into a brine. You can make this the same way, or skip the brine and apply the dry rub to the skin—just don't brine *and* rub the bird, or it will be too salty.

WHOLE CHICKEN

MAKES 4 SERVINGS

1 gallon water

1 cup Fette Sau Dry Rub (page 35)

or

½ cup Fette Sau Dry Rub (page 35)

1 whole chicken (about 4 pounds)

Wood chunks or soaked wood chips

1 *If brining the chicken:* In a stockpot, bring the water and dry rub to a boil, stirring until the sugar and salt are dissolved. Let the brine cool to room temperature, then transfer to a nonreactive container and refrigerate until chilled.

2 Add the chicken to the cold brine and refrigerate for 4 to 8 hours.

3 Set a wire rack on a baking sheet. Remove the chicken from the brine, pat dry with paper towels, and place on the wire rack. Discard the brine. Refrigerate for 6 hours.

4 *If using just the dry rub:* Put the chicken on a rimmed baking sheet and coat the chicken lightly all over with the dry rub (you may not need all of the rub).

5 Preheat a smoker to 225°F or set up a grill for smoking (see page 44 or 47).

6 Place the chicken in the smoker and smoke, maintaining a smoker temperature of between 200° and 225°F, replenishing the wood chunks or chips as needed, until an instant-read thermometer inserted into the center of a leg registers 165°F. Total smoking time will be 3 to 5 hours. Transfer the chicken to a cutting board and let rest for 10 minutes.

7 At this point, you can cut the chicken into quarters or tear the meat into shreds to make pulled chicken. Or, if you want extra-crispy skin, you can briefly roast the chicken in a 450°F oven, or prepare a grill with hot and cool sides, put the chicken over the cool side, cover the grill, and cook for 5 to 10 minutes.

BEEF BRISKET PASTRAMI

We created this pastrami in homage to New York City's most famous deli meat, but it actually more closely resembles the heavily smoked beef found in Montreal. Pastrami is often made with just the first cut of a brisket (also called the flat), but we use the entire thing, which results in meat that stylistically falls between something you'd find piled on rye bread in a deli in New York or Montreal and the plates of smoked brisket served in Texas. Because it takes a couple of weeks to brine this gargantuan piece of meat, this is one recipe for which you'll have to plan ahead.

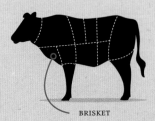

BRISKET

MAKES 10 TO 12 SERVINGS

BRINE

1 gallon water

1 cup kosher salt

1 teaspoon curing salt (see Note, page 37, and Resources, page 255)

1 large Spanish onion, sliced

1 head garlic, halved horizontally

½ cup Pickling Spices (recipe follows), or use a jarred mixture

1 whole beef brisket (10 to 14 pounds)

RUB

1 cup cracked coriander seeds

1 cup cracked black peppercorns

Spicy Mustard (page 114), for serving

Wood chunks or soaked wood chips

① In a container large enough to hold the brisket, combine the water, kosher and curing salts, onion, garlic, and pickling spices and whisk until the salt is dissolved. Add the brisket, cover, and refrigerate for 2 weeks, turning the brisket over periodically if it's not completely submerged.

② In a small bowl, combine the coriander and pepper.

③ Remove the brisket from the brine and pat dry. Trim the fat cap to about ⅛ inch thick, removing any hard lumps of fat. Put the brisket on a rimmed baking sheet and coat all over with the dry rub, patting it onto the surface until the meat has an even layer of rub (you may not need all of the rub). If you have time, let the meat rest for 1 to 2 hours, until the rub starts to moisten and turn into a pasty coating.

④ Preheat a smoker to 225°F or set up a grill for smoking (see page 44 or 47).

⑤ Place the brisket, fatty side up, in the smoker and smoke, maintaining a smoker temperature of between 210° and 225°F, replenishing the wood chunks or chips as needed.

⑥ After about 8 hours, start checking the meat periodically: Poke the brisket in a few places; the fat cap should be soft and pliant and the meat should separate under your finger. If you think your brisket is nearly done, cut off a good chunk and eat it. The bark should be dry and crisp, and the meat should be moist and tender but not mushy or overly chewy. Total smoking time will be 12 to 16 hours.

NOTE:

Brisket is best eaten right away, but if you have to cook it ahead of time, let it cool to room temperature, then wrap it in multiple layers of plastic and refrigerate. To rewarm the brisket, unwrap it and place it in a roasting pan. Add a splash of water and cover with foil, then heat it in a 200°F oven until warmed through. If the bark has gone soft, you can recrisp it over a medium-hot grill fire for a few minutes.

7 When the brisket is smoked to your liking, using two pairs of tongs or a pair of heavy rubber gloves, transfer it to a cutting board. If your cutting board doesn't have a channel for catching juices, put it on a rimmed baking sheet. Let the meat rest for at least 30 minutes.

8 Just before serving (once sliced, brisket dries out quickly), slice the brisket across the grain into ¼-inch pieces, beginning at the thinner end of the cut. When you encounter the thick band of tough fat that separates the point from the flat, cut the remaining brisket into two pieces between the point and the flat. Remove most of the fat, then continue. Serve with the spicy mustard.

PICKLING SPICES

Makes about ½ cup

2 tablespoons mustard seeds

2 tablespoons coriander seeds

2 tablespoons
black peppercorns

1 tablespoon dill seeds

2 teaspoons allspice berries

1 teaspoon red pepper flakes

2 whole cloves

2 bay leaves, crumbled

1 cinnamon stick, smashed
into pieces

Combine all of the spices in a jar. Seal the jar and shake until combined.

BEEF TONGUE PASTRAMI

I grew up eating beef tongue, so it's never been a weird thing for me to cook—but it is one of the more intimidating meats to smoke. It's a slippery, slimy organ meat whose origin is very apparent, but once you get past that part, it's a very tender, tasty cut with a flavor that will remind you of brisket. This preparation is a mash-up of boiled beef tongue and pastrami, and it can be sliced and eaten right out of the smoker like barbecue, or chilled and thinly sliced, charcuterie-style.

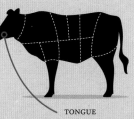

TONGUE

MAKES 10 TO 12 SERVINGS

1 beef tongue (2 to 3 pounds)

BRINE

1 gallon water

1 cup kosher salt

1 teaspoon curing salt (see Note, page 37, and Resources, page 255)

1 large Spanish onion, sliced

1 head garlic, halved horizontally

½ cup Pickling Spices (page 163), or use a jarred mixture

RUB

½ cup cracked coriander seeds

½ cup cracked black peppercorns

Spicy Mustard (page 114), for serving

Pickles, for serving

Wood chunks or soaked wood chips

1 In a large pot, cover the tongue with cold water. Bring to a boil, reduce the heat, and simmer the tongue for 1½ hours.

2 Transfer the tongue to a cutting board. When it is cool enough to handle, peel away the skin.

3 In a container or resealable plastic bag large enough to hold the tongue, combine the water, kosher and curing salts, onion, garlic, and pickling spices and whisk until the salt is dissolved. Add the tongue, cover, and refrigerate for 1 week.

4 In a small bowl, combine the coriander and pepper.

5 Remove the tongue from the brine and pat dry. Put the tongue on a rimmed baking sheet and coat it all over with the dry rub, patting it onto the surface until the meat has an even layer of rub (you may not need all of the rub).

6 Preheat a smoker to 225°F or set up a grill for smoking (see page 44 or 47).

7 Place the tongue in the smoker and smoke, maintaining a smoker temperature of between 210° and 225°F, replenishing the wood chunks or chips as needed, until an instant-read thermometer inserted into the center of the tongue reads 175°F. Total smoking time will be 6 to 8 hours.

8 To serve the tongue warm, thinly slice it across the grain on a bias. Or refrigerate until chilled, then slice as thin as possible. Serve with the spicy mustard and pickles.

BACON

The great thing about making your own bacon is that you're completely in charge of every step of the process: what kind of pork to use, how to flavor the cure, how heavily to smoke the bacon, and how thick to cut it before cooking. Berkshire pigs make my favorite bacon, but feel free to use other heritage breeds: Large Black and Tamworth also produce great bacon. Try substituting maple syrup or honey for the brown sugar, and experiment with other woods for the smoking.

PORK BELLY

While commercial bacon is cold-smoked (at a temperature at or below 140°F), it's risky to cold-smoke meat or fish at home, as some harmful pathogens could survive the process. This bacon is "warm-smoked," just above the cold-smoking threshold, which both speeds up the process and makes it safer.

MAKES ABOUT 4 POUNDS

¼ cup kosher salt

2 teaspoons curing salt (see Note, page 37, and Resources, page 255)

¼ cup packed dark brown sugar

3 tablespoons coarsely ground black pepper

One 5-pound pork belly, skin removed

Applewood chunks or soaked applewood chips

1 In a small bowl, combine the kosher salt, curing salt, brown sugar, and pepper. Put the pork belly on a rimmed baking sheet and cover it with the cure, rubbing it well into the meat and fat (you may not need all of the cure). Wrap the belly in plastic wrap and refrigerate for 7 days.

2 Unwrap the pork belly and rinse off the cure.

3 Preheat a smoker to 140°F or set up a grill for smoking (see page 44 or 47).

4 Place the pork belly in the smoker and smoke, maintaining a smoker temperature of between 140° and 160°F, replenishing the wood chunks or chips as needed, until an instant-read thermometer inserted into the center of the belly registers 140°F. Total smoking time will be 4 to 5 hours. Transfer the bacon to a clean surface and let cool to room temperature.

5 Pat the bacon dry with a paper towel, then wrap in plastic and refrigerate until firm before slicing and cooking. You can also cut the bacon into large slabs, wrap them individually, and refrigerate or freeze. The bacon can be refrigerated for up to 1 week or frozen for up to 2 months.

AN OUTSIDER AT MEMPHIS IN MAY

I've never been interested in competition barbecue. There's something about competitive cooking in general that I can't get behind: why does cooking need to be a sport? It makes about as much sense to me as a competitive painting tournament or battle-royal jazz.

But I couldn't pass up the chance to play pitmaster for a couple of days back in 2009, when the editors of *Men's Health* magazine offered to send me and three other guys from the New York barbecue restaurant scene to compete in Memphis in May, one of the largest and fiercest barbecue competitions in the world. Some 250 teams vie for the top spot (and $100,000 in prize money) in several categories, with an emphasis on pork (ribs, shoulder, and whole hog), along with ancillary categories like poultry, brisket, sauce, and wings.

For most competitors, an invite to Memphis in May means you're a top pitmaster who's won other events. Many teams consist of twenty or more people who "train" together throughout the year, are well traveled on the barbecue circuit, and roll up to the event with massive custom-built smoker rigs; some even have corporate sponsors. Our team, which snuck in through the back door opened by the magazine, consisted of Kenny Callaghan of Manhattan's Blue Smoke; John Stage of the Dinosaur Bar-B-Que restaurants; Craig Samuel, who owns Brooklyn's Smoke Joint; and me. Of our quartet, only Kenny had some competitive barbecue experience; the rest of us were complete newbies. Each of us would work with one meat and would fend for himself throughout the competition. Kenny took on beef brisket, John went with baby back ribs, Craig made prime rib, and I chose chicken.

By the time we got to the event, we knew we were walking into a buzz saw— or perhaps bringing knives to a gunfight. While our competitors unhitched their elaborate bespoke smokers, we set up a small fleet of Weber kettle grills and bullet smokers—the same equipment we use in our own backyards. I still think the best thing about attending a barbecue competition is seeing the insane rigs some of the teams build. I've seen vintage buses, motorcycles, and cars retrofitted into smokers; a smoker shaped like a giant six-shooter; and too many smokers adorned with pig's ears and snouts to count. A barbecue competition is basically a hot-rod show cloaked in sauce and smoke.

Competitive barbecue has a bunch of very particular, sometimes seemingly counterintuitive, rules. For example, everything must be served to the judges in 9-by-9-inch Styrofoam clamshells, yet you are judged on "appearance" for the way you arrange your barbecue in said container, using only parsley or lettuce as your garnish; other adornments are forbidden. Winning a trophy is as much about following these very specific rules as it is about making great-tasting meat, which itself must play to the judges' proclivities; they tend to favor a sticky, heavily sauced style of barbecue.

Our team decided to stick with the styles of barbecue we make back in New York. I wanted my chickens to have the distinctive flavor of Fette Sau's dry rub, but I elected to turn it into a brine instead of applying it to the outside of the

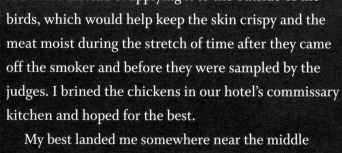

birds, which would help keep the skin crispy and the meat moist during the stretch of time after they came off the smoker and before they were sampled by the judges. I brined the chickens in our hotel's commissary kitchen and hoped for the best.

My best landed me somewhere near the middle of the pack after judging, along with my fellow city-slicker teammates. We were all more than pleased with how our meat turned out, but we knew that it wasn't what the judges were looking for. Despite getting our asses kicked, though, we ended up having a blast: we met a few legendary pitmasters, tasted some amazing barbecue, and had an all-around good hang with people who care as much about smoke and meat as we do.

But I'll probably never do it again.

LESSON NO 14 | DONENESS: KNOW WHERE TO STICK IT

WITH BARBECUE, I usually cook to texture—that is, smoke the meat until it reaches the right balance of tenderness and chewiness that I'm looking for, which varies from cut to cut and animal to animal. But with grilled meats, I almost always cook to temperature. It's the only way to ensure that the meat will be done to your liking. And how you like your meat grilled—just like how long you grow your hair or how milky you take your coffee—is your prerogative and yours only. Don't listen to anyone who says cooking a steak past "black and blue" (charred on the outside, bloody on the inside) is heresy. Likewise, don't sniff at a dinner guest who requests theirs extra-well-done. It's all a matter of personal preference.

For most folks, medium-rare is the default—cooked enough to not worry about your steak running away, not so overcooked as to render it a doorstop. But I have to admit that I like most meat grilled just to the point of medium. Rare meat is too chewy for me—it's like trying to eat a piece of gum. Well-done meat, as we all know, is like chewing leather, and all the flavor has been cooked out. For me, medium offers the best texture, without sacrificing flavor or juiciness.

However you like it, cooking meat to the desired temperature is the hardest part of grilling, period. The difference between perfectly cooked and overdone can be a matter of moments, and any recipe's cooking time suggestions (including my own) are at best rough estimates—so many small and big factors can increase or decrease cooking time that the only way to know when it's done is to find out for yourself.

This, too, isn't as easy as it sounds. Many grilling enthusiasts swear by the "finger test" for determining doneness: you poke at a piece of meat, then poke the palm of your hand at the base of your thumb while pressing various fingers together to find the corresponding firmness. This is supposed to tell you when your meat is cooked to rare, medium-rare, and so on, but I've never understood the reasoning behind this hackneyed method. Different cuts and animals have different textures—a beef tenderloin cooked to medium might feel the same as a rare rib-eye, or a medium-rare pork chop the same as a desiccated chicken breast. Maybe my hands are more or less pudgy than the guy who invented the finger test, but it's never worked for me, at least not consistently.

Other folks use the meat juices as an indicator of doneness. A chicken's juices are said to run clear when it's cooked through, but I've had undercooked chicken ooze clear juices and overcooked chicken run pink; this method is too inconsistent to be trusted. Some cooks will cut into the meat to take a peek inside to check its color. This is also misleading, as meat actually turns redder as it is exposed to oxygen, and

different meats are naturally different shades of red—even within the same type of animal.

What *does* work for me to determine doneness is a good instant-read thermometer. It is accurate and consistent, as long as: (1) your thermometer can be trusted and (2) you know how to use it.

Concerning #1: As "scientific" instruments, most kitchen thermometers are as reliable as a career politician. Cheap thermometers can and will lie to you—or, at best, take too long to tell the truth. But if you find a digital instant-read thermometer that reads temperatures quickly and accurately, you'll never eat an overcooked steak again.

My personal favorite, never-fail thermometer is the Thermapen, made by the British company ThermoWorks (see page 138 and Resources, page 255). There are many cheaper instant-read options on the market and some of these even work well, but you should test any thermometer's accuracy first by dipping it into a pot of boiling water (it should register 212°F within a few seconds) and/or a bowl of ice water (32°F). Anything that takes longer than 5 seconds to display the correct temperature isn't an "instant-read" thermometer and won't serve you well at the grill. If the thermometer is quick but doesn't read the proper temperature, calibrate it (if this is an option) or try another model.

After you've found a thermometer you trust, learn how to use it: Always insert the thermometer into the thickest part of the meat, at least 1 inch away from any bones, which will be hotter than the meat around them. Repeat this in two or three spots near the center to confirm your first temperature reading. (Don't listen to folks who say that this will cause the meat to lose a lot of juices; meat is a sponge, not a balloon, and liquid loss will be minimal unless you treat the meat like a voodoo doll.) With steaks and chops, insert the thermometer through the side; this makes it easier to find the center of the cut. With whole chicken, insert the thermometer between the drumstick and the breast; with chicken breasts, insert the thermometer near the neck cavity into the thickest part of the breast. If you're not confident about the reading, test it again in a different part of the meat.

Keep in mind that meat will continue to cook after you've pulled it off the grill. Depending on the type and cut of meat, the internal temperature will generally rise by somewhere between 5 and 10 degrees as the meat rests, so remove it from the grill *before* it reaches the desired doneness.

THE IMPORTANCE OF RESTING

Resting grilled meat is essential; it lets the meat's muscle fibers relax, which allows its internal juices to be redistributed throughout the cut. Steaks, chops, and chicken parts need about 10 minutes of resting; a large roast or a whole chicken may need 20 minutes or longer. Some recipes tell you to tent resting meats with foil. I almost never do this: while covering meat with foil helps it (slightly) to stay warm, it also creates steam that will ruin the crispy crust or skin that you've worked so hard to obtain. It's better to let your meat rest uncovered, then rewarm it, if necessary, over a low-heat fire or in a warm oven.

GRILLING TEMPERATURES CHART

The chart below gives my recommended cooking temperatures for various cuts of grilled meat. They are typically below USDA recommendations for "safely" cooked meat. As with many things in life, you have to balance safety with pleasure.

	DONENESS	INTERNAL TEMPERATURE (BEFORE RESTING)	USDA–RECOMMENDED INTERNAL TEMPERATURE
BEEF	Rare	115°F	
	Medium–Rare	125°F	145°F
	Medium	135°F	160°F
	Medium–Well	145°F	
	Well Done	155°F	170°F
	Ground Beef	160°F	160°F

	DONENESS	INTERNAL TEMPERATURE (BEFORE RESTING)	USDA–RECOMMENDED INTERNAL TEMPERATURE
PORK AND VEAL	Rare	120°F	
	Medium–Rare	130°F	145°F
	Medium	140°F	160°F
	Medium–Well	150°F	
	Well Done	160°F	170°F
	Ground Pork and Veal	160°F	160°F

chart continues

LAMB	DONENESS	INTERNAL TEMPERATURE (BEFORE RESTING)	USDA-RECOMMENDED INTERNAL TEMPERATURE
	Rare	120°F	
	Medium–Rare	130°F	145°F
	Medium	140°F	160°F
	Medium–Well	145°F	
	Well Done	150°F	170°F
	Ground Lamb	160°F	170°F

POULTRY	DONENESS	TEMPERATURE (OF THE THICKEST PART OF THE THIGH BEFORE RESTING)	USDA-RECOMMENDED INTERNAL TEMPERATURE
	Cooked Through	165°F	165°F

LESSON №15 | GRILLING RED MEAT: COOK TO THE CUT

THERE ARE DOZENS of beef, pork, and lamb cuts appropriate for grilling. But before grilling any piece of red meat, you should know what you're dealing with and adjust your grilling method accordingly. Meat with lots of intramuscular fat—like a beef rib-eye steak or lamb loin chop—is best seared first to get a deep char, then cooked to temperature over lower heat. Thick but lean cuts that carry most of their fat on the outside—like pork chops—benefit from brining or marinating, which helps keep the interior moist as you char the outside. Leaner meats with little marbling or external fat—like veal, beef rump steak, or pork cutlets—should be grilled quickly over a hot fire; by the time they take on a good char, they'll be cooked through.

When choosing meat for grilling, I favor underappreciated, underpriced cuts that most of us tend to overlook in the butcher case. You'll find some of these in the recipes that follow.

BUTCHER'S STEAKS WITH GARLIC BUTTER

The hanger steak (aka butcher's steak) is one of the most underrated cuts of beef. It's silky and fairly tender, thanks to the fact that the muscle, like the tenderloin, does very little work; its primary function is to support the diaphragm. It literally hangs there, from the cow's last rib, unprotected by the bones and fat that surround other cuts. Once the animal is processed, this extra air exposure helps the hanger develop its extra-beefy, almost liver-y flavor. Each cow yields only one (two halves separated by a vein), which means that butchers—back when every neighborhood had one—wouldn't have more than one or two of these steaks on hand at a time, so they'd either grind them into hamburger meat or keep these meat orphans for themselves (hence the name). Its working-class status also makes it the best inexpensive steak around, perfect for a quick weeknight dinner.

HANGER STEAK

On the grill, treat this long, irregularly shaped cut like a sausage, turning it frequently to get a good char on all sides. I prefer mine cooked to medium, which makes it a bit more tender than medium-rare while retaining its gamey flavor and silky texture.

MAKES 4 SERVINGS

Four 10-ounce hanger steaks, trimmed

Kosher salt and freshly ground black pepper

6 tablespoons melted Garlic Butter (recipe follows)

Coarse sea salt

① Prepare a hot single-level fire in a grill (see page 149).

② Generously season the steaks with kosher salt and pepper. Grill the steaks, turning frequently, for about 8 minutes for medium-rare or 10 minutes for medium. Transfer to a cutting board and let rest for 5 minutes.

③ Cut the steaks across the grain on the diagonal into 1-inch slices. Divide among four plates, drizzle with the garlic butter, and sprinkle with coarse salt. Serve.

GARLIC BUTTER

Makes about 1 cup

½ pound (2 sticks) unsalted butter, cubed

6 garlic cloves, finely chopped

① In a saucepan, melt the butter over low heat. Add the garlic and cook over medium-low heat for 5 minutes; the butter should simmer gently but not brown. Remove from the heat.

② Skim the foam from the top of the butter and slowly pour the butter through a fine-mesh sieve set over a bowl. Discard the milky solids and garlic. The butter can be refrigerated for up to 3 weeks.

AXE-HANDLE RIB-EYE STEAK

This beefy behemoth might look and sound intimidating, but it's just like any other rib-eye steak except that it has a full rib attached and it's twice as thick as usual. This is the steak you serve to folks who think they've tried everything a cow has to offer. At St. Anselm, our meat comes from the incredibly marbled American Wagyu cattle at the Masami Cattle Ranch in California. If you have a good butcher and ask nicely, he may be able to prepare one of these for you (many butchers will know this as a "cowboy chop"). If not, ask for a double-cut rib-eye steak and don't worry about skipping the extra length of bone—only your dog will miss it.

RIB-EYE STEAK

When cooking a Flintstones-size steak like this, you have to take extra care to achieve a deeply charred crust and a properly cooked interior. At home, I sear it first, to make sure it gets enough char, then grill it to temperature over low heat. At the restaurant, the cooks do the opposite: they cook the steak over low heat until it reaches 115°F (for medium-rare) and let it rest until they're ready to finish it off, then quickly grill it over scorching-high heat until it's charred all over and serve it immediately—no additional resting necessary. This is what's called a "reverse sear." Use this method if you want to cook your rib-eye up to an hour ahead of time, but be careful to not overcook it during the low-heat phase, or you'll end up with a well-done piece of meat after you sear it.

MAKES 2 TO 4 SERVINGS

One axe-handle rib-eye steak (2½ to 3¾ pounds), about 2 inches thick

Kosher salt and freshly ground black pepper

¼ cup melted Garlic Butter (page 177) or 4 tablespoons unsalted butter, melted

Flaky sea salt, such as Maldon

① Prepare a two-stage fire with high and low sides in a grill (see page 149). Have a spray bottle handy to extinguish any large flare-ups; it's OK for flames to lick the steak now and then, but they shouldn't slobber it with kisses.

② Generously shower the steak with kosher salt and pepper (this will probably be the most you season any piece of meat in your life). Grill the steak over high heat, moving it and turning it every minute or so, until it's well charred on both sides and around the perimeter, 8 to 10 minutes.

③ Move the steak to the low-heat side of the grill and cook until an instant-read thermometer inserted into the center of the meat registers 125°F for medium-rare, 20 to 30 minutes, depending on the size of your steak. Transfer the steak to a platter and let rest for 10 minutes.

continued

4 If the surface of the steak is moist with juices after resting, quickly sear the steak on both sides over high heat to crisp up the crust, about 30 seconds per side.

5 Transfer the steak to a platter. You can either carve the steak as you eat, family–style, or divide it into portions by first cutting the meat away from the bone, then carving the steak across the grain into large pieces. Serve with the melted butter and flaky salt on the side.

NEW YORK STRIP STEAKS WITH SAUCE AU POIVRE

I'll be honest: strip steak is not my favorite cut of beef. Despite its band of external fat, the meat itself isn't terrifically marbled. But I do love its texture, which falls somewhere between that of buttery tenderloin and chewier rib eye—as does the intensity of its flavor. It's such a steakhouse staple that we tried it out at St. Anselm only as an occasional special at first, accompanied by our version of the classic *sauce au poivre*, but high demand quickly made it part of our regular menu. The sauce is proof that pepper brings out the best in red meat, and it also goes well with Charred Long Beans (page 94) and/or Grilled Fingerling Potatoes (page 90).

STRIP STEAKS

MAKES 4 SERVINGS

1 tablespoon extra-virgin olive oil

2 tablespoons very finely chopped shallots

1½ teaspoons coarsely ground black pepper, or more to taste

2 tablespoons apple brandy

2 cups heavy cream

1 tablespoon pink peppercorns

Kosher salt and freshly ground black pepper

Four 13-ounce strip steaks, about 2 inches thick

① Prepare a two-stage fire with high and medium-low sides in a grill (see page 149).

② Meanwhile, in a medium skillet, heat the olive oil over medium-low heat. Add the shallots and cook until translucent, about 5 minutes. Add the coarsely ground black pepper and brandy and carefully tilt the pan slightly away from yourself to ignite the brandy (if you're using an electric stove, carefully light the brandy with a match or a lighter), then cook until the flames subside.

③ Add the cream and pink peppercorns, bring to a simmer, and reduce by half. Season the sauce with more coarsely ground pepper, if necessary, and salt to taste and keep warm over very low heat until ready to serve.

④ Season the steaks generously with salt and freshly ground pepper. Grill the steaks over high heat, turning every couple of minutes, until well charred on both sides, 10 to 12 minutes. Transfer the steaks to the medium-low side of the grill and cook until an instant-read thermometer inserted horizontally into the middle of the steaks reads 135°F for medium, 10 to 15 minutes longer.

⑤ Transfer the steaks to plates and let rest for 5 minutes, then serve with the warm sauce.

BEER-MARINATED RUMP STEAKS

A few years ago, I ran across a recipe for wine-marinated rump steak by Frank DeCarlo, the chef-owner of Manhattan's Peasant and Bacaro restaurants. He'd adapted an ancient Northern Italian recipe for meat marinated in wine and spices for an extended period of time—up to 1 week. I took the idea and made a British version, marinating rump steaks, also known as top round steaks here in the United States, in English imperial stout with spices and citrus zest. Top round is a lean cut often used in braises or roasted whole to make London broil, but it takes well to marinades and packs a lot of flavor for the price. (If you prefer a fattier piece of meat, substitute top sirloin steaks, which will have more marbling.)

Beerwise, any higher-alcohol full-bodied English stout or porter will work, but my favorite for this marinade is imperial stout (aka imperial Russian stout), a style of English beer originally brewed for export to the court of Catherine the Great. It's dark and robust, usually with an alcohol content of about 9 percent ABV. Guinness will not work in this recipe—it's too light and lean—and be careful of American stouts, as many have high amounts of hops, which will make the beef taste bitter.

RUMP STEAKS

MAKES 4 SERVINGS

4 rump (top round) steaks (about 8 ounces each)

24 ounces (3 cups) imperial stout or other full-bodied dark beer

½ teaspoon ground cinnamon

½ teaspoon freshly grated nutmeg

Kosher salt and freshly ground black pepper

3 long strips orange zest

1 Put the steaks in a large resealable plastic bag. Pour the beer into a bowl and, when the foam subsides, whisk in the cinnamon, nutmeg, and ½ teaspoon each salt and pepper. Pour the marinade into the bag, adding as much as necessary to completely cover the steaks, add the orange zest, and seal the bag tightly, squeezing out any extra air as you go. Refrigerate the steaks for 2 to 3 days.

2 Prepare a two-stage fire with medium and low sides in a grill (see page 149).

3 Remove the steaks from the bag; discard the marinade. Pat the steaks very dry with paper towels and season generously with salt and pepper. Grill the steaks over the medium side of the grill, moving and turning them every couple of minutes, until an instant-read thermometer inserted horizontally into the middle reads 135°F for medium, 8 to 10 minutes. If the steaks are well charred before they're ready, move them to the low side.

4 Transfer the steaks to plates and let rest for 5 minutes before serving.

BUTTER-POACHED AND GRILLED BEEF TENDERLOIN STEAKS

Beef tenderloin (aka filet mignon) is unmatched in tenderness, but beyond that, it's a pretty boring cut of beef. It has a mild flavor and is practically devoid of fat, so you really need to do something dramatic to make it worth your trouble (and money). I'm always on the hunt for new cooking experiments, so when I ran across Thomas Keller's recipe for *beurre monté*—an emulsification of butter and a little water that can be warmed to higher temperatures than plain butter without breaking—I thought it would be the perfect way to get me excited about tenderloin again.

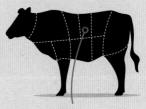

TENDERLOIN STEAKS

At his restaurants, Keller uses *beurre monté* for basting red meats and keeping them warm after they've been cooked to temperature. I reverse the process and poach beef tenderloin steaks in butter until cooked to rare, then finish them over the hottest fire I can build in my grill. The result: a soft-as-ever meat with a crackling-crisp exterior and extra-buttery interior.

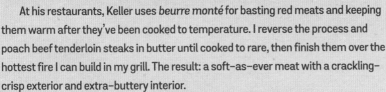

MAKES 4 SERVINGS

2 tablespoons water

1 pound (4 sticks) cold unsalted butter, cut into tablespoon-size pieces

4 beef tenderloin steaks (about 6 ounces each)

Kosher salt and coarsely ground black pepper

> **NOTE:**
>
> The leftover *beurre monté* can be used to poach other meat and seafood. Discard after 1 day.

① In a medium saucepan, bring the water to a boil. Reduce the heat to very low and slowly whisk in the butter a tablespoon at a time, adding another piece only once the previous one has emulsified. The butter will start to look glossy and like hollandaise; if it begins to bubble, remove the pan from the heat to cool slightly before continuing.

② Once all of the butter has been emulsified, add the beef. Use an instant-read or candy thermometer to monitor the *beurre monté*'s temperature: you want to keep it between 140° and 150°F, and you may have to turn off the heat from time to time to prevent it from getting too hot. Cook the beef until an instant-read thermometer inserted horizontally into the center reads 120°F, 20 to 30 minutes. If the beef isn't completely submerged in the butter, turn it over after 10 minutes.

③ Meanwhile, prepare a hot single-level fire in a grill (see page 149).

④ Remove the beef from the *beurre monté*, letting the excess butter drip off, and transfer to a plate. Season the beef with salt and pepper. Grill the steaks, turning once, until charred and cooked to the desired doneness, about 1 minute per side for medium-rare. Transfer to plates and serve.

LAMB SADDLE CHOPS WITH MINT-YOGURT SAUCE

The lamb saddle chop (aka double loin chop or English chop) is an especially succulent (read: fatty) cut that combines the loin and tenderloin, usually with two fatty curlicues hanging off the edges. It's the same cut made famous by Manhattan's Keens Steakhouse, where it's called a mutton chop (though the restaurant hasn't used the older, gamier mutton for years). I love the saddle chop because while most lamb cuts are small and dainty, this one has the same intimidating presence on the plate as a huge steak. To round out the steakhouse experience, serve these chops with the Tomato and Burrata Salad (page 100).

SADDLE CHOPS

MAKES 4 SERVINGS

¾ cup Greek yogurt

¼ cup extra-virgin olive oil

2 tablespoons cider vinegar

2 teaspoons Dijon mustard

2 teaspoons sugar

¼ cup finely chopped mint

Kosher salt and freshly ground black pepper

4 lamb saddle chops (15 to 20 ounces each)

① Prepare a two-stage fire with medium and low sides in a grill (see page 149).

② In a small bowl, whisk the yogurt, olive oil, cider vinegar, mustard, sugar, and mint until combined. Season the sauce to taste with salt and pepper. Refrigerate until ready to serve; the sauce can be refrigerated for up to 1 day.

③ Generously season the lamb all over with salt and pepper. Grill the lamb over medium heat, turning frequently, until well charred on all sides; make sure to grill the fatty edges long enough to render some fat and get them very crisp. Move the lamb to the low side of the grill and cook until an instant-read thermometer inserted into the thickest part of the meat registers 140°F for medium, 15 to 20 minutes. Transfer the lamb to a plate and let rest for at least 5 minutes.

④ Transfer the lamb to plates, spoon some of the yogurt sauce over the chops, and serve.

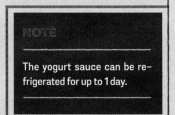

NOTE

The yogurt sauce can be refrigerated for up to 1 day.

LAMB SHOULDER BLADE CHOPS WITH MINT-GREMOLATA BUTTER

The blade chop comes from the rib side of a lamb shoulder, and it is one of the animal's best-kept secrets. But it isn't a cut for beginners: you either have to love eating fat or have a surgeon's knife skills for working your way around it. Either way, you'll be rewarded with one of the juiciest and most intensely flavored (and most economical) cuts of lamb. As soon as the lamb comes off the grill, place a pat of minty compound butter on top, which will melt into the meat as it rests, forming a rich, slightly sweet sauce. Save any leftover butter to top grilled vegetables or an oily fish, such as salmon.

SHOULDER BLADE CHOPS

MAKES 4 SERVINGS

Four 14-ounce lamb shoulder blade chops

Kosher salt and freshly ground black pepper

Four ½-inch disks Mint-Gremolata Butter (recipe follows)

1 Prepare a hot single-level fire in a grill (see page 149).

2 Season the lamb chops generously with salt and pepper. Grill, turning once or twice, until well charred and cooked to the desired doneness, 8 to 10 minutes for medium. Transfer the lamb chops to plates.

3 Place a disk of butter on top of each lamb chop. Let the lamb rest for 5 minutes before serving.

MINT-GREMOLATA BUTTER

Makes about ½ pound

½ pound (2 sticks) unsalted butter, at room temperature

¼ cup finely chopped mint

Finely chopped zest of 2 lemons (about ¼ cup)

1 tablespoon honey

1 teaspoon kosher salt

½ teaspoon freshly ground black pepper

In a food processor, combine the butter, mint, lemon zest, honey, salt, and pepper and pulse until well combined. Transfer the butter mixture to a sheet of plastic wrap and, using the plastic wrap, form it into a log about 2 inches thick. Twist the ends tightly to seal and refrigerate until firm. (The gremolata butter can be refrigerated for up to 1 week or frozen for up to 1 month. Defrost before using.)

VEAL FLANK STEAKS WITH CHIMICHURRI OIL

I always like to introduce people to new parts of an animal to break them out of the habit of eating the same few cuts of meat over and over again. Everyone knows what a veal chop tastes like, so here's a veal flank steak to try instead. It's exactly the same cut as you'd find in beef flank, but it has a much more delicate flavor. The veal flank varies in thickness across the cut, so you want to cook the thickest part of the steak to your desired doneness. If you usually like your steak medium-rare, though, I recommend cooking the veal closer to medium, or it can be chewy. We usually associate chimichurri with hearty Argentinean *asado*, but this simplified version won't overpower the delicate veal. Save any leftover oil to serve with grilled vegetables, such as Grilled Fingerling Potatoes (page 90) or Grilled Fiddlehead Ferns (page 244).

FLANK STEAKS

MAKES 4 SERVINGS

1 bunch parsley

½ cup extra-virgin olive oil

½ cup vegetable oil

3 garlic cloves, roughly chopped

1 tablespoon thyme leaves

Kosher salt and freshly ground black pepper

4 veal flank steaks (5 to 6 ounces each)

1 Bring a saucepan of water to boil. Prepare an ice bath. Blanch the parsley for 15 seconds, then transfer to the ice bath to cool. Drain, squeeze out as much water as possible, and coarsely chop the parsley.

2 In a blender, combine both oils, the garlic, thyme, 1½ teaspoons salt, and ½ teaspoon pepper and blend until the garlic is finely chopped. Add the parsley and blend on low speed until the parsley is finely chopped, then blend on high speed for 4 minutes; the mixture will turn dark green and begin to steam.

3 Line a fine-mesh sieve with cheesecloth and set it over a large measuring cup. Pour the parsley puree into the cheesecloth and let sit until the oil stops dripping (do not press on the solids), about 10 minutes; you should have about ¾ cup oil. The chimichurri oil can be made up to 4 hours ahead.

4 Prepare a hot single-level fire in a grill (see page 149).

5 Generously season the veal with salt and pepper. Grill the steaks, turning once, for 2 to 3 minutes per side, or until the thickest part of the steaks are medium-rare. Transfer the steaks to a cutting board and let rest for 5 minutes.

6 Cut the veal on the bias into ½-inch slices, transfer to plates, drizzle with the chimichurri oil, and serve.

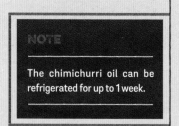

NOTE

The chimichurri oil can be refrigerated for up to 1 week.

LESSON NO 16

GRILLING CHICKEN:
LEAVE IT ON THE BONE

I GRILL A lot of chicken at home, but I can't remember the last time I threw a boneless, skinless chicken breast over the fire—it's basically impossible to make this ubiquitous cut taste good on its own. That's not to say I don't love a good chicken breast: when properly cooked, it can be juicy, meaty, and delicious. But I always leave the breast on the bone, as I do with any piece of chicken. Cooking chicken on the bone both helps the meat hold its shape and prevents it from drying out, and removing the skin both exposes the chicken to more moisture loss and robs you of a delicacy: crispy skin is the best part about eating the bird, no?

Grilling chicken is a race against the clock: the challenge is always to get the meat cooked through before it begins to dry out. White meat (breasts) takes less time to cook than dark meat (legs and thighs). You can, of course, cook breasts and legs separately, but when you want to grill a whole chicken, butterfly it first—that is, remove the backbone with a pair of heavy kitchen shears. Opening the chicken out on the grill not only makes for a more uniform thickness, it also shortens the cooking time and exposes more skin to the hot surface, ensuring that the entire exterior will be crispy by the time the bird is cooked through.

SWEET TEA-BRINED POUSSINS

Poussin is a term for a young chicken, about a month old and weighing in at around a pound. These birds are perfect for grilling: their small, single-serving size makes them cook rather quickly, which keeps the meat moist and tender. If you can't find poussins (or spring chickens, as they're sometimes called) at your market or butcher, grab a Cornish game hen (these are just slightly larger chickens that weigh about 2 pounds), or buy the smallest chicken you can find.

WHOLE POUSSIN

At St. Anselm, we serve locally raised chickens that come with their heads and feet intact. In addition to looking a little scary, it reminds us that what we're eating came from a living, breathing animal and wasn't born in a plastic-wrapped Styrofoam container. Many diners choose to gnaw on the neck and feet, which are quite delicious. You won't often find *truly* whole birds at the market or butcher shop, but if you do, I highly recommend giving it a shot.

Butterflying the birds—by cutting out their backbones with a pair of kitchen shears—speeds up cooking time, but, more important, it exposes more of the chicken to the grill's surface, which helps it reach a deep, even char all over.

MAKES 2 SERVINGS

BRINE

1 gallon water

1½ cups sugar

1 cup kosher salt

3 bay leaves

1 head garlic, halved horizontally

1 medium onion, thinly sliced

1 tablespoon black peppercorns

2 lemons, halved

2 tablespoons tarragon leaves

2 tablespoons parsley leaves

2 black tea bags

① In a stockpot, combine the water, sugar, salt, bay leaves, garlic, onion, and peppercorns. Squeeze the juice of the lemons into the pot and drop in the halves. Bring the mixture to a boil, stir to dissolve the sugar and salt, then turn off the heat. Add the tarragon, parsley, and tea bags and let steep for 20 minutes.

② Remove the tea bags and let the brine cool to room temperature, then transfer to a nonreactive container and refrigerate until chilled.

continued

CHICKEN

2 whole poussins (about 1 pound each), preferably with heads and feet intact (see Resources, page 255), butterflied

Extra-virgin olive oil, for drizzling

Flaky sea salt, such as Maldon

Lemon wedges, for serving

③ Add the poussins to the brine and refrigerate for 3 to 4 hours.

④ Set a wire rack over a rimmed baking sheet. Remove the poussins from the brine and rinse well; discard the brine. Pat the poussins dry with paper towels and place on the wire rack. Refrigerate for 6 hours.

⑤ Prepare a two-stage fire with high and cool sides in a grill (see page 149).

⑥ Place the poussins skin side down, on the hot side of the grill. Grill until dark grill marks form, about 5 minutes. Move the poussins to the low-heat side of the grill, skin side up, cover the grill, and cook until an instant-read thermometer inserted into a leg registers 150°F, about 10 minutes.

⑦ Transfer the poussins to a platter, drizzle with olive oil, sprinkle with flaky salt, and serve with lemon wedges.

A BETTER WAY TO COVER CHICKEN

If you want to speed up the cooking process or use the rest of the grill as the chicken cooks, cover the chicken with a disposable aluminum pan rather than cover the grill entirely, which can sometimes impart a smoky, sooty flavor to the meal.

GRILL-SMOKED CHICKEN WITH JAMAICAN GRAVY

This isn't a recipe for authentic jerk chicken by a long shot: instead of rubbing or marinating the chicken in the traditional seasoning—a lip-numbing blend of allspice, Scotch bonnet peppers, and other ingredients—you smoke the chicken over a mix of wood chips and jerk spices, then serve it with a tangy soy-based sauce infused with Scotch bonnets and allspice berries. The sauce is quite harsh just after it's made, but it will mellow as it ages; so make it at least a day ahead. I keep a bottle in my kitchen and use it for grilled fish as well. If you live near a Jamaican market, you might be able to find some pimento wood sticks or chips (or see Resources, page 255); use them in place of the fruit wood for an even more jerk flavor.

THIGH

MAKES 4 SERVINGS

WOOD CHIP PACKET

¼ cup wood chips, preferably apple or cherry wood, soaked in water for at least 15 minutes and drained

3 tablespoons allspice berries

2 tablespoons dried thyme

2 tablespoons dried rosemary

CHICKEN

8 bone-in, skin-on chicken thighs (about 3 pounds)

Kosher salt and freshly ground black pepper

Jamaican Gravy (recipe follows)

1 Prepare a two-stage fire with medium-high and low sides in a grill (see page 149). Oil the grate well.

2 Place the wood chips in the middle of a 1-foot square of aluminum foil. Sprinkle the allspice berries, thyme, and rosemary over the chips and cover with a second piece of foil. Fold the sides over to make a flat packet about 6 inches square. Using a paring knife, poke holes all over the top of the packet. Place the foil packet on top of the coals in the medium-high side of the grill (or, if using a gas grill, lift the grate and place the foil directly on top of the burner).

3 Season the chicken all over with salt and pepper. When the wood chip packet begins to smoke, place the chicken thighs, skin side down, on the grate over the packet. Grill the thighs, turning them every few minutes, until charred all over and cooked through (an instant-read thermometer inserted into the thickest part of the meat should register 165°F), about 15 minutes. Transfer the chicken to a platter and let rest for a few minutes.

4 Drizzle the gravy over the chicken and serve, passing extra sauce on the side.

continued

JAMAICAN GRAVY

Makes 4 cups

**4 Scotch bonnet or
habanero peppers**

2 cups low–sodium soy sauce

2 cups distilled white vinegar

3 tablespoons allspice berries

① Wearing a pair of latex gloves, cut the peppers into quarters, then remove the seeds and ribs.

② In a jar or an empty wine bottle, combine the soy sauce, vinegar, allspice, and peppers. Seal and shake a few times. Let stand for at least 1 day at room temperature (waiting a week is even better). The sauce's flavor will improve as it stands, and it can be stored at room temperature for several months.

CHICKEN SPIEDIES

BREAST

Spiedies originated in Broome County, New York, an area near the Pennsylvania border that includes the towns of Binghamton and Endicott. It's essentially an Italian–Americanized kebab (the name comes from *spiedini*, the Italian word for skewered meat), made with various types of meat that is marinated and then grilled. A soft roll—or, in some cases, white sandwich bread—is used to pull the grilled meat off the skewer, making for some of the best handheld food around.

    This recipe calls for quotidian boneless, skinless chicken breasts, but you can make spiedies with any kind of tender skewer–friendly cut of pork, lamb, or beef. Marinades vary, but I like to use a homemade Italian dressing; if you have a favorite store–bought brand, feel free to use that instead.

MAKES 6 SERVINGS

2 pounds boneless, skinless chicken breasts, cut into 1-inch cubes

Spicy Italian Dressing (recipe follows)

Kosher salt and freshly ground black pepper

6 soft Italian rolls, split

¼ cup melted Garlic Butter (page 177) or 4 tablespoons unsalted butter, melted

① Put the chicken in a large resealable plastic bag, add enough dressing to cover it, and seal the bag, pushing out any extra air. Refrigerate for at least 4 hours, or as long as overnight.

② Soak 6 long wooden skewers in water for 30 minutes (or use metal skewers). Prepare a medium-hot single-level fire in a grill (see page 149).

③ Thread the chicken onto the skewers and season with salt and pepper. Discard the dressing. Grill the chicken, turning frequently (use tongs; you'll burn your fingers if you try to grab the skewers), until charred all over and cooked through, 8 to 10 minutes.

④ Meanwhile, brush the cut side of the rolls with the melted butter and grill until toasted, 2 to 3 minutes.

⑤ Place a skewer inside each roll and use the bread to hold the meat in place as you pull out the skewer. Drizzle with extra Italian dressing, if desired, and serve at once.

continued

SPICY ITALIAN DRESSING

Makes about 1 ½ cups

½ cup extra–virgin olive oil

½ cup canola oil

¼ cup distilled white vinegar

2 tablespoons red
wine vinegar

2 teaspoons Dijon mustard

1 teaspoon honey

1 garlic clove, finely chopped

1 medium shallot,
finely chopped

3 tablespoons finely
chopped parsley

3 Peppadew peppers,
finely chopped

1 teaspoon kosher salt

¼ teaspoon dried oregano

Pinch of red pepper flakes

Freshly ground black pepper
to taste

Combine all the ingredients in a jar with a lid, cover tightly, and shake well. The dressing can be refrigerated for up to 1 week.

CORNELL CHICKEN

The story goes like this: In the late 1940s, a University of Pennsylvania graduate student named Robert C. Baker was asked to develop a chicken recipe to be served at a dinner attended by the state's governor. He developed an egg-and-vinegar-based emulsion, which he used to marinate and baste halved chickens as they cooked over a charcoal grill. The tangy, juicy, and crispy-skinned chicken was a hit.

A decade later, Baker—then a professor at New York's Cornell University and the school's liaison to local farmers and food marketers—resurrected his recipe as a way to help poultry farmers turn a quicker profit by selling younger (and smaller) broiler chickens. During his tenure, Baker went on to pioneer dozens of ways to package processed poultry, including the chicken nugget and the turkey hot dog. But the barbecue chicken became Baker's most famous contribution. He even published the recipe in an academic journal, declaring that "barbecued broilers without sauce are like bread without butter." Decades later, Baker's "Cornell Chicken" remains a fixture at barbecues, church suppers, and restaurants in the region that encompasses Ithaca and New York's Southern Tier.

The legend of Cornell chicken is one of my favorite barbecue origin stories. I've always wondered why Baker's undeniably delicious recipe hasn't migrated outside of the region. No matter: It's a pilgrimage worth making. My favorite restaurant stop for the bird is Brooks' House of Bar-B-Q in Oneonta (see Resources, page 255), a sprawling complex that cooks its chicken halves on a massive, charcoal-fired indoor pit. The restaurant offers a greatest-hits menu of American 'cue, but the "BBQ chicken dinner" (few establishments actually call it Cornell chicken) is what you come here for.

Other local favorites include Phil's Chicken House in Endicott and Jim's B-B-Q Chicken, an open-air, seasonal restaurant in Candor (see Resources, page 255). But the best place to experience Cornell chicken is to queue up at the many picnics, church barbecues, and fire-department fund-raisers that dominate the weekend social calendar throughout the warm-weather months. Visit this part of New York and look for wisps of white smoke on the horizon; you're sure to find the professor's invention cooking at their source.

CORNELL CHICKEN

More than anything, Cornell chicken shows that new localized styles of barbecue are being invented all of the time—and outside of the South. This crisp-skinned chicken was developed by Dr. Robert Baker, a professor at Cornell University whose poultry innovations also include the chicken nugget and turkey burger (thanks, I guess). This barbecue chicken is marinated in and basted with an acidic mayonnaise-like sauce that helps the skin get extra-crispy on the grill. The recipe below is true to the late Dr. Baker's original spec, though he favored charcoal briquettes over lump charcoal.

MAKES 4 TO 6 SERVINGS

MARINADE
1 large egg
1 cup oil
2 cups cider vinegar
3 tablespoons kosher salt

1 tablespoon Poultry Seasoning (recipe follows)

Two 2½- to 3-pound chickens, quartered

1 In a blender, combine all of the marinade ingredients and blend until smooth, about 30 seconds. (Alternatively, whisk all of the ingredients together in a bowl.)

2 Put the chicken pieces in a large resealable plastic bag, add the marinade, and seal the bag, pushing out any extra air. Refrigerate for at least 3 hours, and as long as overnight.

3 Prepare a two-stage fire with medium-hot and cool sides in a grill (see page 149), making sure to oil the grate well.

4 Remove the chicken from the marinade, letting any excess liquid drip off, and put on a platter or tray. Transfer a cup or so of the marinade to a measuring cup. Place the chicken, skin side down, over the medium-hot side of the fire and cook, turning once, until well charred, about 6 minutes per side. Transfer the chicken to the cooler side of the grill and brush with the reserved marinade. Cover the grill and cook, turning and brushing the chicken with marinade every few minutes (stopping about 5 minutes before the chicken is finished), until an instant-read thermometer inserted into the thickest part of a thigh registers 165°F, 30 to 35 minutes. If the skin isn't crispy, move the chicken to the medium-hot side of the grill and cook it for another minute or so.

5 Transfer the chicken to a platter and let rest for 5 minutes before carving and serving.

POULTRY SEASONING

MAKES 4¾ TEASPOONS

1 teaspoon dried marjoram

1 teaspoon dried savory

½ teaspoon dried parsley

½ teaspoon ground sage

½ teaspoon dried thyme

¼ teaspoon dried tarragon

¼ teaspoon dried rosemary

¼ teaspoon onion powder

½ teaspoon freshly ground black pepper

In a jar, combine all of the spices. Seal the jar and shake to combine. The poultry seasoning can be stored at room temperature for up to 1 month.

LESSON № 17 | GRILLING SEAFOOD: LESS IS MORE

I'VE NEVER MET a piece of fish that didn't benefit from a turn on a hot grill. That said, there are plenty of fish fillets that are too flaky to stand up to the rigors of a live fire. But almost any fish can be grilled whole: the skin protects the delicate flesh and takes to char nicely, as long as your grate is well oiled. With larger fish that are always broken down into smaller cuts, I favor the meatier varieties—like salmon, tuna, and swordfish—and I always opt for grilling steaks over fillets: they're easier to move around the grill, and their uniform size helps them cook more evenly.

Shellfish are my favorite seafood to grill. I throw clams and mussels directly over a hot fire, which steams the meat in its own juices and gives it a slightly smoky flavor. Likewise, crustaceans—shrimp, langoustines, lobster, and the like—have a protective shell that keeps the meat moist and tender and can take a good hit of char.

No matter what kind of seafood you're grilling, keep the preparation simple. A sprinkle of salt and pepper before it hits the grill, a squeeze of lemon juice, and maybe a drizzle of olive oil or melted butter just after it comes off are all good seafood ever needs.

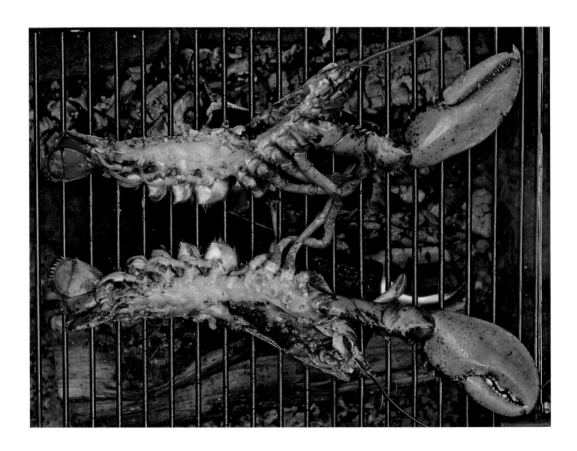

GRILLED SWORDFISH STEAKS WITH WINE-BOTTLE SAUCE

When I'm grilling loads of seafood for a crowd, I'll take a bottle of aromatic dry white wine, drink half of it, and then top the bottle off with olive oil and the juice of a lemon and shake it up (sometimes I add a chopped garlic clove or two and/or a chopped chile). I use this quick concoction three ways: as a marinade, to splash over fish or shellfish as it grills, and as a light, bright sauce. The sauce also works well on any grilled green vegetable, such as Charred Long Beans (page 94) or Charred Broccoli with Pecorino and Lemon (page 97).

Swordfish is at its very best on the grill—it chars easily and absorbs lots of smoky charcoal flavor. Because of its dense, meaty texture, it should be treated more like beef than like salmon or tuna. Buy the thickest steaks you can find—at least 1 inch thick—and cook them to medium, or they will be mushy. A thick swordfish steak can weigh up to a pound, so one steak can serve two people unless appetites are fierce.

MAKES 8 SERVINGS

One 750 ml bottle aromatic dry white wine, such as Sauvignon Blanc

1½ cups extra-virgin olive oil

Juice of 1 lemon

4 swordfish steaks (about 1 pound each), 1 to 1½ inches thick

Kosher salt and freshly ground black pepper

1 Prepare a hot single-level fire in a grill (see page 149).

2 Pour half of the wine (about 1½ cups) into your glass for drinking, and add the olive oil and lemon juice to the bottle. Cover the top of the bottle with your thumb and shake well.

3 Season the swordfish generously with salt and pepper. Grill, turning once and splashing the fish occasionally with the sauce, until charred on both sides and cooked through, 8 to 10 minutes for medium.

4 Transfer the swordfish to plates, drizzle with more wine sauce, and serve. Leftover wine sauce will keep in the sealed bottle in the fridge for up to 1 day.

GRILLED WHOLE TROUT WITH LEMON AND GARLIC BUTTER

Trout has a mild, delicate flavor that really benefits from the smoky heat of the grill. It's also one of the few proteins that you should rub with oil before grilling, as it tends to stick. (Make sure your grill grates are extra clean and well oiled too.) If you want to take this recipe a step further, you can stuff the trout with a few sprigs of your favorite herbs and tie the cavity closed before grilling. Serve the trout atop a simple arugula salad, which will absorb any juices that run out of the fish, creating a delicious dressing.

MAKES 2 TO 4 SERVINGS

2 whole trout, cleaned, scaled, and butterflied (ask your fishmonger to do this)

Extra-virgin olive oil

Kosher salt and freshly ground black pepper

3 tablespoons melted Garlic Butter (page 177)

2 tablespoons chopped parsley

Flaky sea salt, such as Maldon

Lemon wedges, for serving

1 Prepare a hot single-level fire in a grill (see page 149), making sure to oil the grate well.

2 Rub the trout with olive oil and season inside and out with kosher salt and pepper.

3 Grill the trout, turning once, until the skin is crisp and charred and the flesh is opaque throughout, 3 to 4 minutes per side.

4 Transfer the fish to plates and drizzle with the garlic butter. Sprinkle with the parsley and flaky salt and serve with lemon wedges.

GRILLED MACKEREL WITH GREEN PEPPERCORN SAUCE

Oily fish are one of the most forgiving proteins to grill. You don't have to worry about them sticking to the grates, and they're difficult to overcook. Some folks think of mackerel as a pungent fish, but anyone who likes salmon will find a similar flavor profile. (If you come across mackerel that smells "fishy" at the market, don't buy them—they've been out of the water for too long.) Anything pickled pairs well with oily fish: here I use the punchy acidity of pickled green peppercorns (the unripened state of what eventually ends up in pepper mills) to flavor a brown butter sauce, which quickly caramelizes the lime juice and cuts through the richness of the fish. The soy-marinated Grilled Cauliflower (page 248) is a great accompaniment to this dish.

MAKES 4 SERVINGS

4 whole Atlantic mackerel (about 8 ounces each)

Kosher salt and freshly ground black pepper

6 tablespoons unsalted butter

4 sprigs jarred pickled green peppercorns (available at Asian markets)

3 tablespoons fresh lime juice

Flaky sea salt, such as Maldon

Lime wedges, for serving

1 Prepare a hot single-level fire in a grill (see page 149), making sure to oil the grate well.

2 Season the mackerel inside and out with kosher salt and pepper. Grill the fish, turning once, until well charred and cooked through, 4 to 5 minutes per side. Transfer the fish to plates.

3 In a saucepan, melt the butter over high heat. Add the pickled peppercorns and a pinch each of kosher salt and pepper and cook, swirling the pan frequently, until the butter begins to brown, about 6 minutes. Stir in the lime juice (the mixture will bubble up) and simmer until the sauce is syrupy, about 20 seconds.

4 Drizzle the mackerel with the butter sauce and top each fish with a sprig of peppercorn. Sprinkle with flaky salt, and serve with lime wedges.

GRILLED SARDINES WITH PONZU AND PICKLED RED ONIONS

This dish captures the essence of Mediterranean cooking, but it has a noticeably Asian influence. Ponzu is a sweet, tart, and salty Japanese condiment made with rice wine, rice vinegar, bonito, kombu, and citrus (usually yuzu). A quick dip in this vinaigrette-like sauce before grilling helps to cut through the sardines' richness and tame their fishy funk (as do the pickled onions that accompany them). If you can't find ponzu, use fresh lemon juice instead.

MAKES 4 APPETIZER SERVINGS

Eight ½-inch slices crusty bread

Extra-virgin olive oil, for brushing

¼ cup ponzu, plus more for drizzling

8 whole sardines, cleaned and gutted

Flaky sea salt, such as Maldon

Pickled Red Onions (recipe follows), for serving

1. Prepare a hot single-level fire in a grill (see page 149), making sure to oil the grate well.

2. Brush the bread on both sides with olive oil and grill, turning once, until charred on both sides, about 2 minutes. Transfer to a platter.

3. Pour the ponzu into a shallow bowl and add the sardines, turning them to coat. Place the sardines on the grill and cook, turning once, until charred on both sides and opaque in the center, 2 to 3 minutes per side.

4. Transfer the sardines to the platter, drizzle with more ponzu, and sprinkle with salt. Pile the pickled red onions on the platter and serve.

PICKLED RED ONIONS

Makes about ½ cup

1 cup water

½ cup cider vinegar

1 tablespoon sugar

1½ teaspoons kosher salt

1 red onion, halved and thinly sliced

10 black peppercorns

1 star anise

1. In a jar with a lid, combine the water, vinegar, sugar, and salt, cover tightly, and shake until the sugar and salt are dissolved. Add the onion, peppercorns, and star anise and shake again. Let sit at room temperature for 1 hour before using.

2. The onions can be refrigerated for up to 1 week.

GRILLED DIVER SCALLOPS

The most important thing about grilling scallops, as with most seafood, is not to overcook them. You'll notice that this is a very spartan preparation: scallops are so flavorful that you can let them make their own sauce. You don't want to mask their sweet, briny flavor with other ingredients—a touch of smoky char and a sprinkle of salt is all they need. Make sure your grill grate is well oiled; you want that golden, caramelized crust to stay on the scallop, not stick to the grill. Turn the scallops into a main course by serving them with Charred Corn with Compound Cream Cheese (page 103), which pairs marvelously with the shellfish.

MAKES 4 APPETIZER SERVINGS

8 U10 dry-packed diver scallops (about 12 ounces; see Note)

Extra-virgin olive oil

Kosher salt and freshly ground black pepper

Flaky sea salt, such as Maldon

Finely chopped parsley (optional)

1. Prepare a hot single-level fire in a grill (see page 149), making sure to oil the grate well.

2. Lightly brush the scallops with olive oil and season lightly with kosher salt and pepper. Grill the scallops, turning once, until just cooked through, about 1½ minutes per side.

3. Transfer the scallops to a platter and sprinkle with flaky salt. Drizzle with olive oil, sprinkle with parsley, if desired, and serve.

> **NOTE**
>
> The U in U10 stands for "under" and refers to the number of scallops in a pound: U10 means under 10 scallops per pound. These are the largest scallops that you'll encounter at the fish market; if you can't find U10s, buy the largest scallops they have.

GRILLED CLAMS WITH GARLIC BUTTER

I think I grilled my first clams in grade school. Even back then, my Italian friends and I liked to cook in our families' backyards. Our refrigerators were usually stocked with clams or mussels (which work equally well in this recipe), and we were too lazy to run back and forth to the kitchen to cook the shellfish while grilling our burgers and sausages, so we'd just throw the shells on the grill. What's magical about this technique is the smoky flavor the clam liquor picks up from the burning charcoal. You can turn these clams into a main course by serving them with linguine tossed with red pepper flakes, olive oil, and fresh herbs.

MAKES 4 APPETIZER SERVINGS

2 pounds littleneck
clams or cockles (about
2 dozen), scrubbed

3 tablespoons melted Garlic
Butter (page 177)

¼ cup chopped parsley

Freshly ground black pepper

Lemon wedges, for serving

Crusty bread, for serving

1 Prepare a hot single-level fire in a grill (see page 149).

2 Place the clams directly on the grill grates. After 3 to 5 minutes, the clams will begin to open: as they open, using tongs, transfer them to a bowl, being careful not to spill any of their delicious juices. Discard any clams that don't open after 8 minutes.

3 Drizzle the clams with the warm garlic butter, sprinkle with the parsley, and season with pepper. Serve with lemon wedges and crusty bread.

GRILLED MONSTER PRAWNS

If you like grilled lobster tails, you'll love these giant prawns. They have a similar texture to lobster but are more flavorful and less expensive, though they can be harder to find (the prawns I use are from the Gulf of Mexico and are sometimes called Mayan shrimp). And if you're a shrimp-head eater, you'll be rewarded with one of the tastiest slurps you've experienced.

This recipe calls for U4 prawns (meaning 4 prawns or fewer per pound), which might be hard to find except at a good fishmonger. If you can't find them, buy the largest head-on shrimp that they carry and reduce the cooking time by a minute or two.

MAKES 4 APPETIZER SERVINGS

Four U4 prawns (6 to 7 ounces each; see Resources, page 255)

Kosher salt and freshly ground black pepper

¼ cup melted Garlic Butter (page 177)

Extra-virgin olive oil, for drizzling

4 lemon wedges, for serving

1 Prepare a hot single-level fire in a grill (see page 149).

2 Using kitchen scissors, split open the shell of one prawn down the back from head to tail and remove the dark vein with the tip of a paring knife. Repeat with the remaining prawns.

3 Generously season the prawns all over with salt and pepper and grill, turning once, until the shells turn pink, about 3 minutes per side. Then turn the prawns on their backs and grill until cooked through (you'll be able to peek at the flesh through the slit at the base of the head; it should be opaque), about 2 minutes longer.

4 Transfer the prawns to plates and drizzle with the garlic butter and olive oil. Serve with lemon wedges.

GRILLED LOBSTER

Grilled lobster is one of my favorite backyard party foods. I buy enough so each guest gets half a lobster and grill them alongside some quick-cooking steaks, such as the Butcher's Steaks (page 177).

There's no point in grilling lobster, however, unless you let the meat char and absorb some smoky flavor, so I cook them flesh side down first, then turn them over to finish cooking while I baste them with butter. Medium lobsters (about 1½ pounds) are the optimum size for grilling: smaller lobsters cook too quickly and don't have enough time to take on a char, and large lobsters yield tougher meat. When you've finished your lobster feast, save the shells and char them over a hot fire, then use them to make a smoky lobster stock.

MAKES 2 TO 4 SERVINGS

2 live medium lobsters
(1½ pounds each)

½ cup melted Garlic Butter
(page 177)

Kosher salt and freshly ground
black pepper

½ lemon, plus
4 lemon wedges

¼ cup chopped parsley

Flaky sea salt, such as Maldon

1 Prepare a medium-hot single-level fire in the grill (see page 149).

2 To quickly kill the lobsters, place one lobster on a cutting board with its head facing you. Insert the tip of a large chef's knife into the lobster's back about 1 inch behind its eyes, then plunge the knife down to split its head between the eyes. Turn the lobster around and split it in half through the back and tail. Scoop out and discard the dark green roe and the pale green tomalley. Crack the claws by whacking them with the back of the chef's knife. Repeat with the other lobster.

3 Brush the flesh of the lobster halves with some of the garlic butter and season with kosher salt and pepper. Place the lobsters, flesh side down, on the grill and cook until the flesh side is charred, about 3 minutes. Turn the lobsters over, brush the flesh with butter, and continue grilling and basting with butter until the flesh side is opaque and firm to the touch, 3 to 5 minutes longer.

4 Transfer the lobsters to a platter and squeeze the lemon half over them. Sprinkle with the parsley and flaky salt and serve with lemon wedges and any leftover butter.

GRILLED "WHOLE" SALMON

At St. Anselm we buy salmon whole, which means that each fish leaves us with a head and tail (and a collar; see page 220) after we butcher the rest into steaks. We thought it would be cheeky to serve these delicious remnants together, head affixed to tail, and, more important, we didn't want to waste these underrated parts. Like the collar, a salmon's head is rich and fatty, and the tail, while leaner, is one of the most flavorful parts of the fish (your fishmonger should have both hiding in the back of the shop). This is a dish best shared by two folks who won't get scared off by the sight of a fish staring them in the eyes—and who are willing to dig a little with fork and knife to excavate the treasure.

MAKES 2 SERVINGS

1 salmon tail (about 1 pound)

1 salmon head (10 to 12 ounces)

Kosher salt and freshly ground black pepper

3 tablespoons melted Garlic Butter (page 177)

Flaky sea salt, such as Maldon

Lemon wedges, for serving

1 Prepare a two-stage fire with medium and low sides in a grill (see page 149).

2 Season the salmon with kosher salt and pepper. Grill the tail over the medium side of the grill, turning every couple of minutes, until charred and cooked through, 10 to 12 minutes. At the same time, grill the head over the low side until charred and cooked through, about 10 minutes.

3 Transfer the salmon to a plate, placing the head and tail together. Drizzle with the garlic butter, sprinkle with flaky salt, and serve with lemon wedges.

GRILLED SALMON COLLAR

If you like salmon, you will adore salmon collar, an extra-fatty, gnarly looking piece cut from just behind the fish's gills. It's rich, unctuous, and crispy all at once—a giant piece of fish-flavored bacon is the best analogy I can come up with. The first time I tasted it, I thought, *Why haven't I been eating this forever?*

You'll want to cook collar longer than you're used to cooking other cuts of salmon on the grill, as it takes time to render all that fat. As such, salmon collar also loves to catch on fire, so keep a spray bottle handy to extinguish any flare-ups.

Though you may not see it on display, your fishmonger will usually have one or two collars on hand if he buys his salmon whole (as any good market should). Asian fish markets usually have plenty on hand as well. If you can't find salmon collar, hamachi collar (which you can find at Asian markets) is almost as great. A rich fish like this needs a nice crunchy salad to round it out. Serve it with the Iceberg Wedge with Warm Bacon Dressing and Blue Cheese (page 99) or alongside some of my mom's Dilly Coleslaw (page 93).

MAKES 1 TO 2 SERVINGS

One 14-ounce salmon collar

Kosher salt and freshly ground black pepper

2 tablespoons melted Garlic Butter (page 177)

Flaky sea salt, such as Maldon

Lemon wedges, for serving

1 Prepare a two-stage fire with medium and medium-low sides in a grill (see page 149).

2 Season the salmon collar with kosher salt and pepper. Grill the salmon over medium heat, turning every couple of minutes, until charred and cooked through, 10 to 12 minutes. If the salmon is well charred before it's cooked through, move it to the medium-low side of the grill.

3 Transfer the salmon to a plate and drizzle with the garlic butter. Sprinkle with flaky salt and serve with lemon wedges.

LESSON №18 | YOU CAN GRILL BEFORE NOON

ALMOST ANYTHING YOU cook on the stovetop can be moved outside to the grill. While most cooks usually don't fire theirs up until well into the afternoon or evening, I'm fond of grilling in the morning, especially before the heat sets in on scorching summer days. Plus, grilling breakfast or lunch is a great way to use any smoked meat left over from a weekend barbecue. On many a Sunday morning, I'll bring a couple of skillets outside to fry up some eggs, cook some hash, or grill a sandwich.

To me, breakfast is the common denominator in American cuisine: we all eat basically the same stuff—eggs, meat, bread. The same goes for lunch, with sandwiches and salads. And brunch is just a Venn diagram of the two. So whether you're a crack-of-dawn riser or a late sleeper, you can use these recipes as an excuse to start your day in the great outdoors.

GRILLED BERKSHIRE BACON

I borrowed this recipe from Peter Luger, the legendary Brooklyn steakhouse, where grilled strips of extra-thick bacon are served alongside their famous porterhouse steaks. With bacon this thick, it's best to partially cook it in the oven, until the fat turns soft enough to melt in your mouth. Trying to cook it start-to-finish on the grill will result in a lot of flare-ups and sooty-tasting bacon.

Berkshire pigs make the best bacon: their bellies are meatier than other pigs', with evenly distributed fat. Many of the top pork producers offer Berkshire bacon, or you can make your own using the recipe on page 166. Though you can serve it with anything that usually benefits from a side of bacon, this is not your typical breakfast bacon; grab a knife and fork.

MAKES 4 SERVINGS

One 1-pound slab Berkshire bacon, cut into ½-inch slices

① Preheat the oven to 350°F. Set a wire rack over a rimmed baking sheet.

② Arrange the bacon on the rack and bake until some of the fat has rendered and the bacon is golden brown and slightly crispy, 20 to 30 minutes.

③ Meanwhile, prepare a hot single-level fire in a grill (see page 149), making sure to oil the grate.

④ Grill the bacon, turning once, until charred, 2 to 3 minutes per side. Transfer to plates and serve.

STEAK AND EGGS

One of the very first things I cooked for myself—I think I was twelve at the time—was a hamburger patty with a fried egg on top. I've always loved steak and eggs for the way it combines breakfast with dinner. I wouldn't eat this dish at 8 A.M. before work on a weekday, but it's one of my favorite weekend brunches and a great use for leftover meat and potatoes.

Never grilled an egg before? All you do is heat up a skillet on the hottest place possible on the grill and crack the eggs into it. To help the whites set quickly, cover the skillet (or the grill) while the eggs cook.

MAKES 4 SERVINGS

Two 8-ounce hanger steaks, trimmed

Kosher salt and freshly ground black pepper

1 tablespoon vegetable oil

4 large eggs

Grilled Fingerling Potatoes (page 90)

Coarse sea salt

6 tablespoons melted Garlic Butter (page 177)

1 Prepare a hot single-level fire in a grill (see page 149).

2 Generously season the steaks with kosher salt and pepper. Grill the steaks, turning frequently, for about 8 minutes for medium-rare or 10 minutes for medium. Transfer to a cutting board and let rest for 5 minutes, then cut each steak in half.

3 Meanwhile, heat the oil in a large nonstick skillet over the grill. Crack the eggs into the pan and fry until the whites are set but the yolks are still runny, about 4 minutes. Season with kosher salt and pepper.

4 Divide the steaks and potatoes among plates and sprinkle with coarse salt. Top each steak with a fried egg. Drizzle the garlic butter over the steak and eggs and serve at once.

BRISKET HASH WITH FRIED EGGS

It's easy to turn the leftovers from a Saturday barbecue into Sunday brunch. I use smoked brisket here, but you can make this hash with pulled pork, chicken, or rib meat—or whatever other smoked meat remnants you have hanging around.

MAKES 4 SERVINGS

1 pound Beef Brisket (page 64)

4 tablespoons vegetable oil

1½ pounds russet potatoes (4 or 5 medium), peeled and cut into ½-inch dice

¼ teaspoon ground mace (or grated nutmeg)

½ teaspoon garlic powder

½ teaspoon granulated onion

Kosher salt and freshly ground black pepper

2 large garlic cloves, finely chopped

1 red onion, diced

1 red bell pepper, cored, seeded, and diced

1 green bell pepper, cored, seeded, and diced

1 jalapeño pepper, seeded and finely chopped

8 large eggs

1 Trim any large hunks of fat from the brisket and finely chop the fat. Cut the meat into ½-inch pieces, reserving any pieces of fat.

2 Heat 2 tablespoons of the vegetable oil in a large skillet, preferably cast-iron, over medium-high heat and add the chopped brisket fat. When the fat begins to sizzle and melt, add the potatoes in a single layer and cook, without stirring, until they begin to brown on the first side, 4 to 5 minutes. Stir in the mace, garlic powder, and granulated onion, season with salt and pepper, and continue cooking, stirring every few minutes, until the potatoes are tender and golden-brown all over, 8 to 10 minutes longer.

3 Add the garlic, onion, and peppers and cook, stirring frequently, until softened, about 3 minutes. Add the brisket and cook until warmed through. Season the hash to taste with salt and pepper.

4 Meanwhile, heat 1 tablespoon of vegetable oil in a large nonstick skillet over medium-high heat. Crack 4 of the eggs into the pan and season with salt. Cook until the whites are set but the yolks are still runny, 3 to 4 minutes. Repeat with the remaining tablespoon of oil and the remaining eggs.

5 Divide the hash among plates, top each with 2 fried eggs, and serve.

GRILLED ROMAINE SALAD

This salad is a cross between a Grilled BLT (page 231) and a classic Caesar salad. Romaine is the best lettuce for grilling: it can withstand the heat, and it really benefits from a deep char, as it absorbs the grill's smoky flavor.

MAKES 4 TO 6 SERVINGS

4 romaine lettuce hearts

Extra-virgin olive oil, for brushing

Kosher salt and freshly ground black pepper

Caper-Anchovy Dressing (recipe follows)

4 slices Grilled Berkshire Bacon (page 223), cut crosswise into ¼-inch-wide strips (lardons)

2 cups Bacony Croutons (recipe follows)

Pickled Red Onions (page 210)

4 hard-boiled eggs, halved

A chunk of Parmigiano-Reggiano cheese, for shaving

① Prepare a medium-hot single-level fire in a grill (see page 149).

② Cut the romaine hearts lengthwise in half, leaving the cores intact. Brush on both sides with olive oil, then season with salt and pepper. Grill the lettuce, cut side down, until well charred, about 2 minutes, then turn over and grill until slightly wilted, 1 to 2 minutes longer.

③ Transfer the lettuce to a platter and drizzle with the dressing to taste. Scatter the bacon, croutons, and pickled onions over the top and arrange the eggs on the salad. Shave the cheese over the top and serve.

continued

CAPER-ANCHOVY DRESSING

Makes about 1 cup

2 anchovy fillets

1 tablespoon Dijon mustard

1½ teaspoons sherry vinegar

2 large egg yolks

¼ cup canola oil

¼ cup extra-virgin olive oil

2 teaspoons capers, finely chopped

1 teaspoon finely chopped shallot

Kosher salt and freshly ground black pepper

Put the anchovies on a cutting board and use a fork to mash them into a paste. Transfer to a bowl and whisk in the mustard, vinegar, and egg yolks. Slowly whisk in the canola oil, followed by the olive oil, until the dressing is thick and emulsified. Stir in the capers and shallot and season to taste with salt and pepper. The dressing can be refrigerated for up to 1 day.

BACONY CROUTONS

Makes about 2 cups

2 cups cubed country bread (1-inch pieces)

1 tablespoon extra-virgin olive oil

1 tablespoon warm bacon fat

Kosher salt and freshly ground black pepper

① Preheat the oven to 375°F.

② In a medium bowl, toss the bread with the olive oil and bacon fat. Spread the bread on a baking sheet and season with salt and pepper. Bake, turning the croutons over every few minutes, until golden brown, 10 to 15 minutes. Let cool.

GRILLED BLT WITH PICKLED TOMATOES AND AVOCADO SPREAD

I came up with this recipe while spending a weekend at a house in Asbury Park, New Jersey. It was so nice outside that I didn't want to cook brunch indoors, so I gathered the ingredients for a BLT and stationed myself at the grill.

Use extra-thick-cut bacon here: thinner slices will be harder to grill, as they like to curl up from the heat and will cook unevenly. If you only have thin bacon, press the slices flat against the grill with a baking sheet or skillet as they cook. The pickled tomatoes make this a year-round BLT, but if you find yourself in the middle of tomato season, by all means use fresh tomatoes.

MAKES 4 SERVINGS

4 tablespoons unsalted butter, at room temperature

8 slices Pullman loaf or 4 hamburger buns

¼ cup Garlic Aioli (recipe follows)

¼ cup Avocado Spread (recipe follows)

Eight ½-inch slices slab bacon

2 romaine lettuce hearts, cut lengthwise into quarters (cores left intact)

Vegetable oil, for brushing

4 jarred pickled green tomatoes, cut into ½-inch slices

4 fried eggs (optional)

1 Prepare a medium-hot single-level fire in a grill (see page 149), making sure to oil the grate well.

2 Butter the bread on both sides and grill, turning once, until toasted on both sides, 1 to 2 minutes per side. Spread 1 tablespoon of the aioli on each of 4 slices of bread and spread 1 tablespoon of the avocado spread on the other slices.

3 Grill the bacon, turning often, until crispy and charred in spots, 4 to 6 minutes.

4 Brush the lettuce with oil and grill, cut side down, until lightly charred, 15 to 20 seconds.

5 Place the lettuce on top of 4 slices of the bread. Top with the tomatoes, bacon, and fried eggs, if using. Top the sandwiches with the remaining bread and serve.

continued

GARLIC AIOLI

Makes about ½ cup

1 garlic clove, halved and germ removed

Kosher salt

1 large egg yolk

1 teaspoon Dijon mustard

¼ cup extra-virgin olive oil

¼ cup vegetable or canola oil

2 teaspoons fresh lemon juice

Freshly ground black pepper

AVOCADO SPREAD

Makes about 1½ cups

2 ripe avocados

5 ounces cream cheese, at room temperature

¼ cup crème fraîche

3 tablespoons Garlic Aioli (above)

2 tablespoons fresh lemon juice

Kosher salt and freshly ground black pepper

① Using the side of a heavy knife, mash the garlic clove and a pinch of salt into a paste on a cutting board. Transfer to a bowl, add the egg yolk and mustard, and whisk together.

② Combine the oils in a measuring cup and begin to add the oil to the egg yolk mixture a few drops at a time, whisking constantly until emulsified. Then continue whisking while slowly adding the remaining oil. (If the aioli begins to separate, stop adding oil and whisk until it comes back together, then proceed.) Whisk in the lemon juice and season the aioli to taste with salt and pepper. If it's too thick, thin with a few drops of water. Refrigerate until ready to serve. The aioli can be refrigerated for up to 2 days.

Halve and pit the avocados and scoop the flesh into a bowl. Mash well with a fork. Add the cream cheese, crème fraîche, aioli, and lemon juice and whisk until smooth. Season to taste with salt and pepper. Use immediately.

GRILLED PATTY MELT WITH CARAMELIZED ONIONS

The patty melt combines all the best qualities of hamburgers (juicy ground beef), sliders (caramelized onions), and grilled cheese (bread and melted cheese).

A lot of people obsess over the blend of beef in their burgers, but I think the cut (or cuts) you choose isn't nearly as important as fat content: you want your burgers to be 80 percent lean (meat) and 20 percent fat. Use the highest-quality ground beef you can find. Or, if you have your butcher grind the meat to order, choose brisket, chuck, hanger steak, short rib, skirt steak, or sirloin: These cuts—or some combination thereof—all make excellent burgers. Brisket happens to be my favorite burger meat; it has a good fat content and loads of flavor.

MAKES 4 SERVINGS

CARAMELIZED ONIONS

2 tablespoons olive oil

1 medium onion, thinly sliced

1 bay leaf

Kosher salt and freshly ground black pepper

2 tablespoons dry white wine

2 pounds 80% lean ground brisket (or your favorite beef cut or cuts)

Kosher salt and freshly ground black pepper

Softened butter for the bread

8 slices seeded rye bread (about ¾ inch thick)

8 slices Emmenthaler cheese

Pickles, for serving

1. In a large skillet, heat the olive oil over medium heat. Add the onions and bay leaf and sprinkle with salt and pepper. Cover and cook, stirring occasionally, until the onions are golden and softened, about 15 minutes.

2. Uncover the skillet and add the wine. Bring to a simmer, scraping up any browned bits on the bottom of the pan, and cook until no liquid remains, about 2 minutes. Season to taste with salt and pepper and set aside. Remove the bay leaf before serving.

3. Prepare a two-stage fire with high- and low-heat sides in a grill (see page 149), making sure to oil the grates well.

4. Put the ground beef in a bowl and season generously with salt and pepper. Form the beef into 4 patties, each about 1 inch thick.

5. Grill the patties on the hot side of the grill, turning once, about 2 minutes per side for medium-rare. Transfer to a plate.

6. Butter one side of a piece of bread. Place a grilled patty on the unbuttered side and top with some of the caramelized onions, then cover with 2 slices of cheese. Top with another slice of bread and butter it. Repeat with the remaining ingredients to make 4 patty melts.

7. Grill the sandwiches on the low-heat side of the grill, turning once, until the bread is toasted, about 2 minutes per side. Cut the patty melts in half diagonally and serve with pickles.

GRILLED SAUSAGE, PEPPER, AND ONION SANDWICHES

I generally recommend the hot variety over sweet sausage in this classic Italian-American sandwich. The best way to grill sausages is to lay them parallel to the grill grates so they nestle in between the bars—this gives you maximum casing-to-grill contact. Whatever you do, don't turn the sausages with a fork as they cook; this will puncture the skin, letting fat (and flavor) ooze out and create flare-ups.

For extra heat, grill some pickled hot chile peppers (the long green ones from a jar) alongside the sausages, and add one to each sandwich. Save any leftover peppers and onions for scrambled eggs the next day.

MAKES 4 SERVINGS

1 large red onion, cut into ½-inch slices

½ cup extra-virgin olive oil, plus more for brushing

Kosher salt and freshly ground black pepper

2 green bell peppers

2 red bell peppers

¼ cup balsamic vinegar

4 hot or sweet Italian sausages (or a mix)

4 Italian hoagie or submarine rolls, split

4 jarred pickled hot chile peppers (optional)

1 Prepare a two-stage fire with hot and medium sides in a grill (see page 149).

2 Brush the onion slices on both sides with olive oil and season with salt and pepper. Arrange the onion slices over the medium side of the fire and grill, turning once, until lightly charred and softened, about 10 minutes. Meanwhile, put the peppers on the hot side and grill, turning occasionally, until blistered and charred all over, about 10 minutes. Transfer the peppers and onions to a cutting board and let cool slightly.

3 Cut the onion slices into quarters and transfer to a medium bowl. Peel the peppers (it's OK—even preferable—to leave some of the charred skin attached) and discard the cores, seeds, and ribs. Cut the peppers into long ½-inch-wide strips and add them to the bowl with the onions. Add the oil and vinegar, season with salt and pepper, and toss well.

4 Cook the sausages on the hot side of the grill, turning them every couple of minutes, until browned all over and cooked through (an instant-read thermometer inserted into the center should read 160°F), about 8 minutes. If the sausages brown too quickly, move them to the medium side of the grill.

continued

(5) Meanwhile, brush the cut sides of the rolls with olive oil and toast on the medium side of the grill until browned, about 5 minutes. If using, grill the hot chile peppers on the medium side of the grill, turning once, until lightly charred, about 1 minute.

(6) Place a sausage in each roll and top with some of the pepper and onion mixture, and a chile pepper, if using. Serve.

LESSON №19 | A GRILL BASKET IS YOUR BUDDY

I'M NOT MUCH for grilling gadgets, but there's one piece of equipment that can be a game-changer: the grill basket. This simple tool lets you bring so much more to the grill, including small or skinny ingredients—green beans, Brussels sprouts, diced vegetables, shrimp, and so on—that would otherwise slip between the grates and perish in the fire below.

Grill baskets come in an array of shapes and sizes, but my workhorse basket looks like a skillet made of wire mesh, which allows for the most contact between the food and the grill (and exposure to grill smoke). It has a long handle, which allows me to effectively sauté over a live fire. Some grill baskets are made of metal punched with holes or slits, but these don't allow maximum charring.

Other grill baskets are designated specifically for whole fish. These make grilling fish easier by preventing the skin from sticking to the grates, but you'll lose some of that flavorful char, and a properly oiled grill (see Lesson #12, page 151) should never fail you. There is one style of grill basket that I love using for seafood, however: a lidded rectangular basket. It can hold a lot of shellfish for an easy mixed grill (see page 247).

Grill baskets are also an excellent tool for cooking over a camp fire or in your fireplace. You can use them like a portable grill grate to cook just about anything over a fire.

GRILLED SHISHITO PEPPERS

One of my favorite childhood smells was the earthy, smoky scent of bell peppers being roasted over an open stovetop flame. My grandparents always had strips of roasted peppers marinating in olive oil and vinegar, ready to serve with just about anything. When grilled, shishito peppers—the Japanese cousin of the Spanish Padrón pepper—acquire that same lovely flavor, though eating them can be a game of chance: most shishitos are mild, but about one in ten will smack you in the mouth with a spicy surprise.

MAKES 4 APPETIZER SERVINGS

20 shishito peppers

2 tablespoons olive oil

Kosher salt and freshly ground black pepper

Flaky sea salt, such as Maldon

Lime wedges, for serving

1. Prepare a hot single-level fire in a grill (see page 149).

2. In a bowl, toss the peppers with the olive oil until well coated. Season with kosher salt and pepper.

3. Place a grill basket on the grill and add the peppers. Grill, tossing frequently, until blistered all over and charred in a few spots, 2 to 3 minutes.

4. Transfer the peppers to a platter and sprinkle with flaky salt. Serve with lime wedges.

GRILLED FIDDLEHEAD FERNS WITH CURED HAM

Fiddleheads—the unfurled shoots of new ferns—are one of the first announcements of spring. With an earthy, asparagus-like flavor and a crunchy texture, they are a delicacy that can only be enjoyed for a few weeks each year, right around the time it's finally warm enough to fire up the grill. Look for them at your local farmers' market or a gourmet grocery store.

MAKES 4 SIDE-DISH SERVINGS

1 pound fiddlehead ferns

2 tablespoons extra-virgin olive oil

Kosher salt and freshly ground black pepper

2 tablespoons melted Garlic Butter (page 177)

8 thin slices prosciutto, speck, or other cured ham, diced

2 tablespoons finely chopped mixed tarragon, chives, and parsley

1 Bring a large pot of salted water to a boil. Prepare an ice bath. Add the fiddleheads to the boiling water and blanch for 1 minute, then shock in the ice water until cool. Drain and pat dry with paper towels.

2 Prepare a hot single-level fire in a grill (see page 149).

3 In a bowl, toss the fiddleheads with the olive oil. Season with salt and pepper.

4 Transfer the fiddleheads to a grill basket and grill, tossing frequently, until charred all over, about 4 minutes.

5 Transfer the fiddleheads to a serving bowl and drizzle with the garlic butter. Add the diced prosciutto and herbs, toss well, and serve.

GRILLED ARTICHOKE HEARTS WITH AIOLI

Grilling jarred artichokes is about as quick and simple as an appetizer/side dish can get. Just make sure to use oil-packed artichokes, not the ones in brine, which have too much water to benefit from the grill. If you don't feel like making aioli, squeeze a lemon over the grilled artichokes and call it a day.

MAKES 4 APPETIZER OR SIDE-DISH SERVINGS

12 jarred marinated artichoke hearts (packed in oil), drained and cut lengthwise in half

½ cup Garlic Aioli (page 233)

1 lemon

2 tablespoons chopped parsley

Coarsely ground black pepper

1 Prepare a medium-hot single-level fire in a grill (see page 149).

2 Place the artichokes, cut side down, in a grill basket. Grill until charred on the first side, about 2 minutes, then flip and char the other side, about 2 minutes longer.

3 Transfer the grilled artichokes to plates and spoon some of the aioli over them. Finely grate some lemon zest over the top and sprinkle with the parsley and pepper. Serve immediately.

SEAFOOD MIXED GRILL

This recipe requires a box-like grill basket fitted with a lid, which is something you should own if you like to grill a lot of seafood. It is my favorite way to grill seafood for a crowd: everything cooks together rather quickly in the basket and then, once dumped onto a platter, forms a spectacular sauce as the juices mingle with olive oil and lemon. Treat this recipe as a template: you can mix and match the fish and shellfish you want to use, but just make sure to choose seafood that will cook in roughly the same amount of time. And have plenty of bread on hand for sopping up the sauce.

MAKES 4 SERVINGS

2 pounds assorted shellfish (such as U16 shrimp, dry-packed diver scallops, langoustines, and/or mussels) and firm white fish fillets (such as mullet, halibut, or tilapia), cut into 2-inch pieces

¼ cup olive oil, plus more for drizzling

Kosher salt and freshly ground black pepper

1 lemon, thinly sliced, plus ½ lemon

A handful of mixed herb sprigs, such as tarragon, parsley, and chives, plus scallions

Crusty bread, for serving

1 Prepare a medium-hot single-level fire in a grill (see page 149).

2 In a bowl, toss the seafood with the olive oil and season with salt and pepper.

3 Open a grill basket (see the headnote) and place it on the grill. Scatter the seafood evenly over the bottom of the basket. Lay the lemon slices over the seafood and scatter the herbs on top. Drizzle the herbs with olive oil. Grill, without moving the basket, for 4 minutes, then flip the basket over and squeeze the lemon half over the seafood. Continue cooking until the seafood is opaque and cooked through, about 4 minutes longer.

4 Carefully open the basket and pour the contents into a shallow bowl or onto a platter. Drizzle with olive oil and serve with crusty bread.

GRILLED CAULIFLOWER

Any cruciferous vegetable tastes better with some char on it. Here, cauliflower's natural sweetness is boosted by dousing it in a quick salty–sweet marinade. This technique works equally well with broccoli, but be sure to cook either vegetable until just crisp–tender, with a little bit of bite.

MAKES 4 APPETIZER OR SIDE-DISH SERVINGS

3 tablespoons tamari

3 tablespoons balsamic vinegar

1 tablespoon extra–virgin olive oil, plus more for drizzling

1 head cauliflower (about 2 pounds), cored and cut into 1–inch florets

Kosher salt

1 tablespoon finely chopped parsley

Flaky sea salt, such as Maldon

① Prepare a hot single–level fire in a grill (see page 149).

② In a large bowl, whisk together the tamari and vinegar. Slowly whisk in the olive oil. Add the cauliflower and toss until well coated. Season lightly with kosher salt.

③ Place a grill basket on the grill and add the cauliflower. (If your grill basket isn't large enough to hold the cauliflower in a single layer, cook it in two batches.) Grill the cauliflower, tossing frequently, until crisp–tender and caramelized all over, 10 to 12 minutes.

④ Transfer the cauliflower to a platter. Drizzle with olive oil, sprinkle with the parsley and flaky salt, and serve.

LESSON Nº 20 | WINE SHOULD MAKE A STATEMENT

THE MARVELOUS THING about pairing wine with grilled foods is that the flavor of char works equally well with white and red wines (and anything in between). As with beer, I don't have any secrets or hard-and-fast rules about pairing wine and food: I either follow the normal food-pairing conventions—red wine with red meat, white wine with white meat and seafood, rosé with everything—or, more often than not, just open a bottle of whatever I'm in the mood to drink.

On the other hand, wine is quite difficult to pair with barbecue. Although barbecue is usually fatty and rich, it can easily be overpowered by a big red, and the spices in dry rubs and barbecue sauces—along with their inherent sweetness and heat—tend to clash with wine of any style or color. One exception I've discovered is off-dry sparkling wine, including Champagne and bubbly reds such as Lambrusco or sparkling Shiraz; these have the bubbles to cut through the richness of the fatty meat and the sweetness to complement the rubs and sauces.

I am, however, highly selective when choosing wine to drink with a meal, and I'm always on the hunt for something distinct and different. Whenever I taste a new wine, I ask myself, does this wine make a statement? Does it surprise and excite me? Is it made honestly? The last thing I want to drink is a wallflower wine that tastes like everything else. Stylistically, my preferences range from bold, heady reds to lean and light whites to intense, idiosyncratic Champagnes—pretty much anything intriguing enough to command my attention that also has some semblance of acidity. I tend to gravitate toward wine made from obscure or almost-forgotten grapes, winemakers who buck traditional techniques or use minimal intervention in the winery, and producers from underappreciated wine regions or who fly under the radar in more famous areas. I'm also always on the hunt for the gulpable, easy-drinking wines known as *vins de soif*—literally, "thirst wines." These wines, usually whites and rosés, and lighter-bodied reds, are especially easy to pair with food and intriguing enough to beckon you back to the glass after every sip.

I try to pay as little attention to the price of wine as possible: I've found just as many expressive bottles for $15 as I have at ten times as much. But my proclivity for the underdog or the obscure usually leads to my finding a tremendous value. As a result, it may appear that I assemble a wine list quite recklessly, loading it with every interesting bottle I encounter and being more concerned about how the wines stand on their own and less about how they pair with steaks and seafood. But it's not that food-friendliness doesn't come into play. Wine should never get in the way of what you're eating.

Here are some of my favorite producers, loosely grouped into categories (though many fit into more than one). Many of these wines aren't made in mass-market quantities and can take some searching to find, but they're well worth the hunt.

AMERICAN MAVERICKS

I respect New World producers who are more concerned with growing the right grapes for the environment than with growing what's expected or popular in their region. The winemakers behind these labels love to use obscure grapes; pioneer new vineyard locations and rehabilitate old, long-forgotten vineyards; experiment in the winery; and use their independence and small size to their advantage. Whereas larger producers usually dump or sell wine that doesn't work out as planned, these independent producers have the freedom to see if time or tinkering can make a misfit wine even better—and it often does. Some of them, especially Sean Thackrey and Bedrock Wine Co., are playing a major role in discovering and rehabilitating old vineyard sites and grape varieties.

* **Anthill Farms**
  (Healdsburg, California)
* **Arizona Stronghold/**
  Caduceus Cellars
  (Arizona)
* **Arnot-Roberts**
  (Healdsburg, California)
* **Bedrock Wine Co.**
  (Sonoma, California)
* **Broc Cellers**
  (Berkeley, California)
* **Channing Daughters**
  (Long Island, New York)
* **Donkey and Goat**
  (Berkeley, California)
* **Forlorn Hope**
  (Napa, California)

* **Matthiasson**
  (Napa, California)
* **Red Hook Winery**
  (Brooklyn, New York)
* **Salinia Wine Company**
  (Santa Rosa, California)
* **The Scholium Project**
  (Napa, California)
* **Sean Thackrey**
  (Bolinas, California)
* **Sky Vineyards**
  (Glen Ellen, California)
* **Teutonic Wine Company**
  (Portland, Oregon)
* **Turley Wine Cellars**
  (Templeton, California)

MINIMALISTS

This group encompasses a wide variety of styles, but these producers all make highly drinkable wines using minimal intervention in both the vineyard and the winery. In the vineyard, they usually follow organic and biodynamic viniculture practices. In the winery, they let wild yeast lead the fermentation and they typically don't filter, fine, or sulfur their wines. In some cases, they even use old techniques like packing wine in clay amphorae and fermenting white wines with their skins left on. These are all signifiers of what's become known as "natural winemaking," though I'm hesitant to use the term when describing these winemakers because so much natural wine is flawed in one way or another. Some of these winemakers are young upstarts and others are old-school producers, but they all are masters at producing distinctive bottles.

* **Andrea Calek** (Rhône, France)
* **Angiolino Maule** (Veneto, Italy)
* **Clos du Tue-Boeuf** (Loire Valley, France)
* **Domaine Mosse** (Loire Valley, France)
* **Frank Cornelissen** (Sicily, Italy)
* **Julien Courtois** (Loire Valley, France)
* **Louis-Antoine Luyt** (Maule Valley, Chile)
* **Paolo Bea** (Umbria, Italy)
* **Radikon** (Friuli, Italy)
* **Tenute Dettori** (Sardegna, Italy)
* **Les Vins Contés/Olivier Lemasson** (Loire Valley, France)

GROWER CHAMPAGNE

I got into Champagne rather reluctantly. It was my least favorite style of wine for a long time—but then I realized I was just drinking the wrong Champagne. I was introduced to grower Champagne, and everything changed. In the Champagne district, the number of grape growers far outweighs the number of wine producers; the industry is dominated by a handful of large houses (Krug, Moët & Chandon, Pol Roger, and so on). But some of the viticulturists there decided to make their own small-batch Champagnes. When you don't have a giant brand that you need to support globally, you can take chances that the big guys can't. The result is a huge variety of distinctive sparkling wines made by experimenting with grape ripeness, aging techniques, and more. Some grower Champagne producers like René Geoffroy opt for an intense, lush, hedonistic style, while others, like Pierre Peters, aim for a more graceful, elegant, classic profile. Finding a grower Champagne at the wine shop is easy if you're lucky enough to find a shop that carries them in the first place:

just look for the letters RM (*Récoltant-Manipulant*) on the label. You can drink most Champagne with anything, and some funkier, rustic bottles or very rich styles will pair with everything straight through your meal.

* Agrapart
* A. Margaine
* Chartogne-Taillet
* Egly-Ouriet
* Emmanuel Brochet
* Gaston Chiquet
* Henri Goutorbe
* Paul Bara
* Pierre Gimonnet & Fils
* Pierre Peters
* René Geoffroy
* Vilmart & Cit

THE JURA

The Jura is a tiny French valley between Burgundy and Switzerland. There a unique style of white wine is produced using a technique similar to that for making sherry, in which wines are allowed to age in the barrel under a protective layer of yeast, rather than get topped off by other wine to prevent oxidation. The nutty, aged flavors that result make wine geeks swoon. But I've grown to love the region's red wines as well. Mostly based on Pinot Noir, Poulsard, and/or Trousseau, these light-bodied reds are highly aromatic and fun to pair with foods that we usually eat with white wine.

* André et Mireille Tissot
* Château d'Arlay
* Jacques Puffeney
* Jean-François Ganevat
* L'Octavin
* Peggy et Jean-Pascal Buronfosse
* Philippe Bornard
* Rolet Père et Fils
* Stéphane Tissot

BURGUNDY OUTLIERS

Though I love Burgundian Pinot Noir and Chardonnay and drink as much as I can afford (which isn't much), I've found wines from Burgundy's less-famous regions—reds from Beaujolais and whites from Chablis and Mâconnais—that are equally as good at a fraction of the price. A great cru Beaujolais will bring you as much joy as a Burgundian Pinot, and a top Chablis or Mâconnais can taste better than a great Chardonnay.

* Château Fuissé (Pouilly-Fuissé)
* Damien Coquelet (Beaujolais)
* Diochon
* Domaine de la Cedette
* Georges Descombes
* Guffens-Heynen (Pouilly-Fuissé)
* Guy Breton
* Jean Foillard (Beaujolais)

* Jean-Paul Thévenet
  (Beaujolais)
* Julie Balagny

* Maison Verget
  (Mâconnais/Chablis)

* Marcel Lapierre
  (Beaujolais)
* Robert-Denogent

UNDER-THE-RADAR REGIONS

These winemakers are big fish in small ponds; they make the best wines in regions
that aren't on most drinkers' minds when they buy wine. Most produce both
inexpensive, everyday wines and pricey special-occasion bottles, making them
the best names to start with when introducing yourself to the treasures of Serbia,
Lebanon, or the lesser-known corners of Italy, France, or Austria.

* **Argiolas** (Sardinia, Italy)
* **Ar.Pe.Pe.** (Valtellina, Italy)
* **Castello dei Rampolla**
  (Chianti, Italy)
* **Château de Pibarnon**
  (Bandol, France)
* **Château Musar** (Bekaa
  Valley, Lebanon)

* **Domaine Comte Abbatucci**
  (Corsica, France)
* **Domaine Olga Raffault**
  (Chinon, France)
* **Edi Simčič**
  (Dubrovo, Slovenia)
* **Endrizzi** (Trentino, Italy)
* **Gerhard Pittnauer**
  (Burgenland, Austria)

* **Milijan Jelić** (Pocerina,
  Serbia)
* **Occhipinti** (Sicily, Italy)
* **Vino Budimir**
  (Župa, Serbia)
* **Wine & Soul** (Douro
  Valley, Portugal)

UNDER-THE-RADAR PRODUCERS

Here are smaller fish in big ponds, producers you don't hear about as much as other
producers in their region. But they consistently make excellent wine in price ranges
that always offer a value.

* **Behrens Family Winery/
  Erna Schein** (St. Helena,
  California)
* **Cave Yves Cuilleron**
  (Rhône, France)
* **Château de Saint Cosme**
  (Rhône, France)
* **G. D. Vajra**
  (Piedmont, Italy)

* **Herman Story** (Central
  Coast, California)
* **Inama** (Friuli, Italy)
* **K Vintners/Charles Smith
  Wines** (Walla Walla,
  Washington)
* **Quinta do Infantado**
  (Duoro, Portugal)

* **R. López de Heredia**
  (Rioja, Spain)
* **Weingut Loimer**
  (Kamptal, Austria)
* **Weingut Matthias Dostert**
  (Mosel Valley, Germany)

RESORCES

BOOKS

What follows is a pretty random selection of reference books and cookbooks that I've used over the years to inspire my cooking and further my beer, wine, and spirits education. Some of these books are obscure and/or out of print, so you might have to hunt around if you're interested in reading them.

MEAT, BUTCHERY, AND CHARCUTERIE

Applestone, Joshua, and Jessica Applestone. *The Butcher's Guide to Well-Raised Meat.* Clarkson Potter, 2011.

Farr, Ryan. *Whole Beast Butchery.* Chronicle Books, 2011.

Fearnly-Whittingstall, Hugh. *The River Cottage Meat Book.* Ten Speed Press, 2007.

Grigson, Jane. *The Art of Charcuterie.* Knopf, 1968.

Kaminsky, Peter. *Pig Perfect.* Hyperion, 2005.

Wilson, Tim, and Fran Warde. *The Ginger Pig Meat Book.* Lyons Press, 2011.

GRILLING

Eds. of *Cook's Illustrated* Magazine. *The Cook's Illustrated Guide to Grilling and Barbecue.* America's Test Kitchen, 2005.

Mallman, Francis, and Peter Kaminsky. *Seven Fires: Grilling the Argentine Way.* Artisan, 2009.

Raichlen, Steven. *The Complete Illustrated Book of Barbecue Techniques.* Workman, 2001.

BARBECUE HISTORY AND LORE

Berry, Wes. *The Kentucky Barbecue Book.* University Press of Kentucky, 2013.

Caldwell, Wilber W. *Searching for the Dixie Barbecue: Journeys into the Southern Psyche.* Pineapple Press, 2005.

Elie, Lolis Eric. *Smokestack Lightning: Adventures in the Heart of Barbecue Country.* Ten Speed Press, 2005.

Garavini, Daniel, and Gabriele Roveda. *Pigs and Pork.* Könemann, 1999.

Garner, Bob. *North Carolina Barbecue: Flavored by Time.* John F. Blair, 1996.

Mills, Mike, and Amy Mills. *Peace, Love & Barbecue.* Rodale, 2005.

Moss, Robert F. *Barbecue: The History of an American Institution.* University of Alabama Press, 2010.

Staten, Vince, and Greg Johnson. *Real Barbecue.* Globe Pequot Press, 2007.

Walsh, Robb. *Barbecue Crossroads: Notes and Recipes from a Southern Odyssey.* University of Texas Press, 2013.

HISTORIC COOKBOOKS

Child, Lydia Maria Francis. *The American Frugal Housewife.* Forgotten Books, 2012.

Estes, Rufus. *Rufus Estes' Good Things to Eat.* Dover Publications, 2004.

Fisher, Abby. *What Mrs. Fisher Knows About Old Southern Cooking.* Kessinger Publishing, 2012.

Hagen, Ann. *A Handbook of Anglo-Saxon Food.* Anglo-Saxon Books, 1998.

Nathan, Joan, and Esther Levy. *Mrs. Esther Levy's Jewish Cookery Book.* Andrews McMeel Publishing, 2012.

Plymouth Antiquarian Society. *The Plimoth Colony Cook Book.* Dover Publications, 2005.

Price, B. Byron. *National Cowboy Hall of Fame Chuck Wagon Cookbook.* Hearst Books, 1995.

Simmons, Amelia. *American Cookery.* Tredition Classics, 2013.

FOOD, TRAVEL, AND REFERENCE

Katz, Sandor Ellix. *Wild Fermentation.* Chelsea Green Publishing, 2011.

Mariani, John. *The Dictionary of American Food & Drink.* Hearst Books, 1995.

Stern, Jane. *The Lexicon of Real American Food.* Lyons Press, 2011.

Stern, Jane, and Michael Stern. *500 Things to Eat Before It's Too Late.* Houghton Mifflin Harcourt, 2009.

———. *Roadfood.* Clarkson Potter, 2014.

AMERICAN COOKING

America's Test Kitchen. *The Complete America's Test Kitchen TV Show Cookbook 2001–2014.* Boston Common Press, 2013.

Beard, James. *Beard on Food.* Bloomsbury, 2008.

Choate, Judith, and James Canora. *Dining at Delmonico's.* Stewart, Tabori & Chang, 2008.

Cook's Country. *The Complete Cook's Country TV Show Cookbook.* Boston Common Press, 2012.

Cunningham, Marion. *The Fannie Farmer Cookbook: Anniversary Edition.* Knopf, 1996.

Shopsin, Kenny, and Carolynn Carreño. *Eat Me: The Food and Philosophy of Kenny Shopsin.* Knopf, 2008.

Stern, Jane, and Michael Stern. *American Gourmet.* Perennial, 1992.

BEER

Aidells, Bruce, and Denis Kelly. *Real Beer & Good Eats.* Knopf, 1992.

Baron, Stanley Wade. *Brewed in America.* Literary Licensing, 2012.

Jackson, Michael. *Michael Jackson's Great Beers of Belgium.* Brewers Publications, 2008.

Mosher, Randy. *Radical Brewing.* Brewers Publications, 2004.

Oliver, Garrett. *The Brewmaster's Table.* Ecco, 2005.

Renfrow, Cindy. *A Sip Through Time: A Collection of Old Brewing Recipes.* Cindy Renfrow, 1995.

Smith, Gregg. *Beer in America: The Early Years— 1587–1840.* Brewers Publications, 1998.

WINE

Asimov, Eric. *How to Love Wine: A Memoir and Manifesto.* William Morrow, 2012.

Bonné, Jon. *The New California Wine.* Ten Speed Press, 2013.

Lynch, Kermit. *Adventures on the Wine Route: A Wine Buyer's Tour of France.* North Point Press, 1990.

McInerney, Jay. *Bacchus and Me: Adventures in the Wine Cellar.* Lyons Press, 2000.

———. *A Hedonist in the Cellar: Adventures in Wine.* Knopf, 2006.

———. *The Juice: Vinous Veritas.* Knopf, 2012.

Rosenthal, Neal. *Reflections of a Wine Merchant.* North Point Press, 2009.

Standage, Tom. *A History of the World in 6 Glasses.* Walker & Company, 2005.

Thiese, Terry. *Reading Between the Wines.* University of California Press, 2010.

AMERICAN WHISKEY

Cowdery, Charles K. *Bourbon, Straight: The Uncut and Unfiltered Story of American Whiskey.* Made & Bottled in Kentucky, 2004.

Gabanyi, Stefan. *Whisk(e)y.* Abbeville Press, 1997.

Waymack, Mark H., and James F. Harris. *The Book of Classic American Whiskeys.* Abbeville Press, 1997.

TOOLS, ACCESSORIES, AND INGREDIENTS

Most of the gear and tools you need for live-fire cooking can be found at your favorite kitchen or hardware store, but some specialty ingredients, meats, and seafood might be harder to find in your town. Use these resources to order them online.

GRILLING AND BARBECUE TOOLS

SUR LA TABLE
surlatable.com
*Grilling tools
and accessories*

THERMOWORKS
thermoworks.com
*Instant-read thermometers
and digital timers*

WILLIAMS–SONOMA
williams-sonoma.com
*Grilling gear and
grill baskets*

GRILLS AND SMOKERS

BRINKMANN
brinkmann.net
Grills and smokers

CAMERONS
cameronsproducts.com
Stovetop smokers

GRILLWORKS
grillery.com
*Argentinean-style
wood grills*

HOME DEPOT
homedepot.com
*Grills, smokers,
accessories, and fuel*

SPITJACK
spitjack.com
*Tuscan grills
and rotisseries*

WEBER
weber.com
*Grills, smokers,
and accessories*

CHARCOAL AND WOOD

B&B CHARCOAL
bbcharcoal.com
Lump charcoal and wood

PIMENTO WOOD
pimentowood.com
*Pimento chips, sticks,
and charcoal*

THE WOODMAN LLC
thewoodman.com
*Cooking wood
and accessories*

INGREDIENTS

BO BO POULTRY
bobochicken.com
*Rare-breed chickens,
guinea hens, and poussins*

FOSSIL FARMS
fossilfarms.com
Exotic meats and game

GREAT ALASKA SEAFOOD
**great-alaska-
seafood.com**
*Prawns, lobster, salmon,
and other seafood*

HERITAGE FOODS USA
heritagefoodsusa.com
*Heritage-breed pork, beef,
lamb, goat, and poultry*

MURRAY'S CHEESE
murrayscheese.com
*Halloumi, burrata, and
other specialty cheeses*

PENZEYS SPICES
penzeys.com
*Spices and salts, including
curing salt*

RANCHO GORDO
ranchogordo.com
*Pinquito and other
heirloom beans*

BARBECUE RESTAURANTS

CALIFORNIA (SANTA MARIA BARBECUE)

FAR WESTERN TAVERN
300 E. Clark Avenue
Orcutt, CA
farwesterntavern.com

THE HITCHING POST I
3325 Point Sal Road
Casmalia, CA
805-937-6151
hitchingpost1.com

JOCKO'S STEAK HOUSE
125 N. Thompson
    Avenue
Nipomo, CA
805-929-3565

SANTA MARIA ELKS LODGE
1309 N. Bradley Road
Santa Maria, CA
santamariaelks.com

SHAW'S RESTAURANT
714 S. Broadway
Santa Maria, CA
805-925-5862

KENTUCKY (MUTTON AND SLICED PORK SHOULDER)

COLLINS BARBECUE
531 East Main Street
Gamaliel, KY
270-457-2828

FRANCES' BAR-B-CUE
418 East Fourth Street
Tompkinsville, KY
270-487-8550

MOONLITE BAR-B-Q INN
2840 W. Parrish Avenue
Owensboro, KY
270-684-8143
moonlite.com

OLD HICKORY BAR-B-QUE
338 Washington Avenue
Owensboro, KY
270-926-9000
oldhickorybar-b-q.com

MARYLAND (PIT BEEF)

CHAPS PIT BEEF
5801 Pulaski Highway
Baltimore, MD
410-483-2379
chapspitbeef.com

PIONEER PIT BEEF
1600 North Rolling Road
Woodlawn, MD
410-455-0015

NEW JERSEY

HENRI'S HOTTS BARBEQUE
1003 Black Horse Pike
Folsom, NJ
609-270-7268
**henrishottsbarbeque
.com**

UNCLE DEWEY'S OUTDOOR BBQ PAVILION
6931 Route 40
Mizpah, NJ
609-476-4040
uncledeweys.com

NEW YORK (CORNELL CHICKEN)

BROOKS' HOUSE OF BAR-B-Q
5560 State Highway 7
Oneonta, NY
607-432-1782
brooksbbq.com

JIM'S B-B-Q CHICKEN
20 Foundry Street
Candor, NY
607-659-4181

PHIL'S CHICKEN HOUSE
1208 Maine Road
Endicott, NY
607-748-7574
philschickenhouse.com

TEXAS (BARBACOA)

VERA'S BACKYARD BAR-B-QUE
2404 Southmost Road
Brownsville, TX
956-546-4159

MY RESTAURANTS

FETTE SAU
354 Metropolitan
    Avenue
Brooklyn, NY
718-963-3404
fettesaubbq.com

FETTE SAU PHILADELPHIA
1208 Frankford Avenue
Philadelphia, PA
215-391-4888
fettesauphilly.com

ST. ANSELM
355 Metropolitan
    Avenue
Brooklyn, NY
718-384-5054

SPUYTEN DUYVIL
359 Metropolitan
    Avenue
Brooklyn, NY
718-963-4140
spuytenduyvilnyc.com

ACKNOWLEDGMENTS

JOE CARROLL

First off, I would like to thank my grandmother Cora and grandfather Dante for teaching me that food is about so much more than just eating—and for making me grate pounds of cheese, crank out yards of pasta, and clean oceans' worth of squid every weekend.

Mom and Dad, thank you for nurturing my love of food by taking me to great restaurants and letting me order anything and everything I wanted, from frogs' legs to escargot to that huge, expensive lobster at Lundy's when I was just six years old.

To my friends from Dumont, New Jersey, and my cousins from all over: thank you for being the brothers I never had.

A huge thank-you to my wife, Kim, for supporting my many odd interests and notions, and, even more so, for encouraging them. Without you standing beside me, there'd be no Spuyten Duyvil, Fette Sau, or St. Anselm. To my twins, Dante and Susannah, thank you for bringing me more joy than I ever thought possible.

To my entire staff, thanks for understanding what it is I'm trying to do (not an easy task) and for being so incredibly loyal—especially Andy and Fontaine, without whom I would never have been as successful.

Thanks to my co-author, Nick Fauchald, who made this book happen; to William Hereford, who made it look great; and to my agents, David Larabell and David Black, for getting it.

Finally, thanks to Judy Pray and everyone at Artisan for giving us the opportunity to share our passion.

NICK FAUCHALD

Joe, long before we met and decided to write a cookbook, you'd already shaped the way I ate and drank. I had never paid much attention to beer until I first stepped into Spuyten Duyvil back in 2003, and I didn't catch the barbecue bug until I had my first bite of a Fette Sau rib while celebrating my birthday there in 2007 (it remains my favorite spot for birthday dinners). Your curious connoisseurship has since introduced me to so many new things—in food and beverage, of course, but also in music, art, and beyond—especially during the writing process. Thanks for holding the bar high and for always doing so in your own unique way.

Thanks to the staffs at Spuyten Duyvil, Fette Sau, and St. Anselm for all of your help—especially chef Katrina Zito, for standing at the hot grill during photo shoots and answering a million recipe questions, and Fontaine Toups and Krystal Lemons, for all of the scheduling, sourcing, and wrangling help.

Rotem Raffe, your artwork and design skills helped us sell this book, and your patience and encouragement helped keep me sane throughout the process. And thanks for always being hungry for more meat.

Thank you, Will Hereford, for the gorgeous photos and for being a fun road-tripper. (Same to you, brother Saint.) And to Rebekah Peppler and Martha Bernabe, for styling and propping much of the food seen here.

A big thanks to the folks at Artisan for (to borrow Joe's words) "getting it," especially our editor, Judy Pray, and copy editor, Judith Sutton.

The hugest thanks to my agents, David Black and David Larabell, for playing matchmaker, salesman, drinking buddy, health coach, taskmaster, and more. This book would have never happened without you.

INDEX